Barriers to Higher Education

A College Entrance Examination Board Colloquium
held at Wingspread, Racine, Wisconsin
June 24–25, 1970

College Entrance Examination Board, New York, 1971

Copies of this book may be ordered from Publications Order Office, College Entrance Examination Board, Box 592, Princeton, New Jersey 08540. The price is $3.50.

Editorial inquiries concerning this book should be directed to Editorial Office, College Entrance Examination Board, 888 Seventh Avenue, New York, New York 10019.

Contents

Authors   iv

Foreword
Stephen J. Wright   v

Educational Opportunity and the Organization of Higher Education
Warren W. Willingham   1

Uses and Abuses of Scholastic Aptitude and Achievement Tests
B. Alden Thresher   24

Response to B. Alden Thresher's Paper
Alexander W. Astin   41

Open Admissions: Status, Trends, and Implications
Timothy S. Healy   44

Response to Timothy S. Healy's Paper
John D. Millett   53

Predicting College Success of Educationally Disadvantaged Students
Julian C. Stanley   58

Response to Julian C. Stanley's Paper
Kenneth B. Clark   78

Personal and Institutional Assessment: Alternatives to Tests
of Scholastic Aptitude and Achievement in the Admissions Process
Winton H. Manning   81

Response to Winton H. Manning's Paper
Hugh W. Lane   100

Programs and Practices for Minority Group Youth in Higher Education
Edmund W. Gordon   109

Response to Edmund W. Gordon's Paper
Helen S. Astin   127

Lack of Money: A Barrier to Higher Education
Humphrey Doermann   130

Colloquium Participants   148

Authors

Alexander W. Astin
Director of Research, American Council on Education

Helen S. Astin
Director of Research, University Research Corporation

Kenneth B. Clark
President, Metropolitan Applied Research Center, Inc.

Humphrey Doermann
Assistant Dean for Financial Affairs, Harvard University

Edmund W. Gordon
Chairman, Department of Guidance, Teachers College, Columbia University

Timothy S. Healy
Vice Chancellor for Academic Affairs, City University of New York

Hugh W. Lane
President, National Scholarship Service and Fund for Negro Students

Winton H. Manning
Director, Developmental Research, Educational Testing Service

John D. Millett
Chancellor, Ohio Board of Regents

Julian C. Stanley
Professor of Psychology, The Johns Hopkins University

B. Alden Thresher
Director of Admissions Emeritus, Massachusetts Institute of Technology

Warren W. Willingham
Senior Research Psychologist, College Entrance Examination Board

Stephen J. Wright
Vice President, College Entrance Examination Board

Foreword

As a part of its continuing effort to help eliminate the enormous deficit in the number of minority/poverty youth who go on for higher education, the College Entrance Examination Board, with the assistance and cooperation of the Johnson Foundation, conducted a Colloquium on Barriers to Higher Education. The purpose of this Colloquium was to examine, critically, the major barriers that stand between the great majority of the blacks, chicanos, Puerto Ricans, and American Indians and equal access to higher education.

The Colloquium, held at Wingspread, the home of the Johnson Foundation, in June 1970, brought together some 50 educators from 20 states and the District of Columbia. The deliberations were organized around seven major, barrier-oriented papers—five of which were responded to, in shorter papers, by scholars who held somewhat different views.

It is becoming increasingly clear that the organization of higher education can be either a barrier to or a facilitator of access to higher education. This problem of the relationship of organization to access has received too little systematic attention from educators. Warren Willingham, Senior Research Psychologist of the College Entrance Examination Board's Access Research Office who has done considerable research in this area, was, therefore, asked to examine the organization of higher education as a barrier. His paper "Educational Opportunity and the Organization of Higher Education," based upon his research, provides sufficient evidence to suggest to educational planners that the organization of higher education is a critical factor in any programs designed to equalize access to higher education for minority/poverty students.[1]

Tests, and especially tests of scholastic aptitude, have long been considered by many, and particularly by members of minority/poverty groups, to constitute one of their major barriers to higher education. Three major papers and three responding shorter papers were, therefore, addressed to this barrier: B. Alden Thresher's "Uses and Abuses of Scholastic Aptitude and Achievement Tests," Julian Stanley's "Predicting College Success of Educationally Disadvantaged Students," and Winton H. Manning's "Personal and Institutional Assessment: Alternatives to Tests of Scholastic Aptitude and Achievement in the Admissions Process." In brief, Thresher holds that it is the *abuse* of aptitude and achievement tests on the part of colleges and universities especially in relationship to irrelevant and unresponsive curriculums that

---

1. See Willingham's *Free-Access Higher Education*. New York: College Entrance Examination Board, 1970, for a fuller treatment of this subject.

constitutes the real barrier. Alexander W. Astin's responding paper essentially agrees with the Thresher position. In brief, Stanley holds that standardized tests and high school grades predict as well for disadvantaged students as they do for regular students. Kenneth B. Clark, who did the responding paper, disagrees with several of Stanley's points. Manning's paper, with its intriguing proposal, "ACORN 80," holds that needed new instruments for both personal and institutional assessment, experimentation on a large scale, and the implementation of the results of the experimentation are the most promising ways to provide alternatives to tests of scholastic aptitude and achievement. Hugh Lane's responding paper presents an argument for a higher priority for education and for open admissions as the real alternative to tests of scholastic aptitude and achievement as presently used.

Admissions standards and policies have obviously constituted a major barrier for many minority/poverty students. Agitation, primarily on the part of minority groups, has been steadily increasing during the past several years. The City University of New York has adopted a form of open admissions. Thus, Timothy S. Healy, Vice President for Academic Affairs of this system, was asked to deal with open admissions as a way of eliminating the barrier of elitist admissions standards and policies. His paper, "Open Admissions: Status, Trends, and Implications," provides an assessment of a major system's efforts to implement a new open admissions policy. The responding paper, by John D. Millet, Chancellor of the Ohio Board of Regents, assesses open admissions in a state that has had such a policy for some 57 years.

In a sense, the paucity of adequate special programs conducted by the institutions of higher learning and related organizations for the purpose of facilitating the admission and retention of minority/poverty youth has constituted a major barrier. Edmund W. Gordon, Chairman of the Department of Guidance at Teachers College, Columbia University, and co-author with Doxey A. Wilkerson of *Compensatory Education for the Disadvantaged,*[2] was asked to inventory and assess programs that have successfully involved the admission and retention of minority/poverty youth. His paper, "Programs and Practices for Minority Group Youth in Higher Education," gives a low rating to existing programs and practices and then proceeds to make specific suggestions for more viable approaches to the problems involved in the admission and retention of minority/poverty youth. Helen S. Astin who responded to Gordon's paper did not take fundamental issue with his position.

Perhaps the greatest of the barriers for minority/poverty youth is the barrier of money. Humphrey Doermann, Assistant Dean for Financial Affairs of the

2. Published by the College Entrance Examination Board in 1966.

Faculty of Arts and Sciences at Harvard, was asked to prepare a paper on "Lack of Money: A Barrier to Higher Education." Doermann suggests a framework for appraising the kinds of students who participate least in higher education and the amount of money they need in order to do so, delineates the issues involved and proposes an addenda.

If one were to attempt to summarize the sense of the lively and sometimes heated discussion that followed the presentation of these papers, the key words would be "change" and "more." Change the use being made of tests of scholastic aptitude and achievement from screening to educational; change the nature of the educational experience the college provides from one intended for an elitist student population to one responsive to the needs of a much more representative group of American youth; change the attitude of faculties toward minority/poverty youth from one of tolerance or even hostility to one of humanness; change the rigid, four-year requirement for graduation to a more flexible pattern in which students proceed at their own pace; change the policy of selective admissions to open admissions. The emphasis on "more" was equally insistent: more truly free-access institutions strategically located; more effective compensatory and supportive programs; more relevant research on the teaching-learning process; more reliable data on the performance of "high risk" students; more, much more, financial aid for the economically disadvantaged student, if he is to have equal access to higher education.

The papers that constitute this volume deal with some of the most critical and urgent problems involved in equalizing opportunity for the minority/poverty groups in the United States. And it is hoped that these papers will not only stimulate national discussion and consideration of the problems but will assist educational policy makers, administrators, and teachers in their efforts to find solutions. Indeed, it should not be too much to hope that many will share the concern of George H. Hanford who opened the Colloquium with these quoted words: "Anger and urgency assail me as I read these excellent papers — anger that so rich and fat a country as ours, dedicated to the worth of the individual personality, should still, so desperately late in history, be starving the educational and personal development of tens of thousands of able children whose only fault is that they are poor, or a wrong color . . . ."

The Colloquium was organized and managed by a Committee consisting of Albert G. Sims, Vice President for Programs, Sam Kendrick, Executive Director of Research, and the writer who served as Chairman.

Many individuals helped to make the Colloquium an educative and stimulating experience: the authors of the papers for taking their assignments seriously, George H. Hanford, Executive Vice President of the College Entrance Examination Board and at that time also acting president, for his counsel and his stage-setting opening remarks, Leslie Paffrath, President of the Johnson Foundation (and his staff) for financial support and the many courtesies that assured the comfort of all participants, Miss Elva Jovisich, Special Assistant to the Vice President for Programs for her excellent staff work, and Mrs. Jane Jacqz for her service as rapporteur.

Stephen J. Wright, College Entrance Examination Board
Vice President

January 1971

Educational Opportunity
and the Organization of Higher Education

By Warren W. Willingham

Throughout this century progressively larger proportions of 18-year-olds have continued education beyond high school. But in the convulsive 1960s enrollment more than doubled and college attendance became the statistical norm for the first time.[1] Access to higher education is increasingly associated with social and economic opportunity in the public mind, and partly for that reason, there is also an urgent effort to achieve a more proportionate enrollment of minority/poverty youth in higher education. These rising expectations have tended to support the attitude that higher education is a right, not a privilege.

The implications of such public expectations are exceedingly complex and often controversial. There has been more than usual attention to such matters as: Who goes to college? (Folger and Nam, 1967); What are the barriers? (Ferrin, 1970); Does education actually yield social opportunity? (Jencks, 1968); What programs can help to improve educational opportunity? (Carnegie Commission, 1970). A collection of recent papers has explored in some detail the resources required for greatly broadened postsecondary education (United States Office of Education, 1970). In contrast, the papers of this particular conference are especially relevant to the role of the institution, particularly the relationship of its policies and practices to expanding educational opportunity.

These policies and practices exist in a larger framework — the overall organization of higher education. What is the relationship between opportunity and organization? That is the basic question to which this paper is addressed. We begin by assuming that the conditions of educational opportunity are imbedded

---

1. According to the latest information available, the ratio of first-time college students to 18-year-olds is .53; the corresponding figure a decade earlier was .36. (*Opening Fall Enrollment, 1958, 1968;* U.S. Bureau of the Census, 1970.)

in legislation, master plans, and facilities, in organizational relationships and programs, and in the collective policies and practices — all institutionalized in an overall system widely understood to be variegated and complex if not incomprehensible.

It is hardly possible to discuss the organization of higher education without giving due attention to its basic nature and function. This is especially true since the intersection of opportunity and organization is fundamentally a social and political matter that touches all significant aspects of the educational process. In very limited space any discussion of these matters is likely to be superficial; nonetheless some context is necessary in order to gain full benefit from subsequent descriptive material.

Consequently, this paper comes in three parts. The first part is concerned with the current meaning of educational opportunity and major issues involved in its implementation. The second part reports briefly some findings from a national study of the extent to which higher education is accessible to various populations. Finally, I shall draw upon this information in describing the organization of accessible higher education in various states, particularly as it bears upon the major issues outlined.

What Does Opportunity Mean?

Coleman (1969) notes that the idea of educational opportunity is evolutionary; through time it has tended to take on additional characteristics so that the concept is broadened. A single inexpensive, nonselective university in a state was once regarded as an advanced egalitarian expression of equal opportunity. A recent statement by the Carnegie Commission (1970) captures well a more current interpretation. It states, "The transcendent goal is that inequality in one generation should not, inevitably, be a legacy of succeeding generations." Income, ethnic group, geographic location, age, and quality of early schooling were cited as examples of characteristics or conditions that at this time discriminate in the education opportunity of individuals. (Interestingly, sex was not included.)

There seem to be three principal assumptions underlying this statement and similar ones issued by earlier commissions (Eisenhower Commission, 1960; Educational Policy Commission, 1964). First, no artificial barriers such as money or geography should inhibit educational aspiration. The question of what is artificial will likely be debated and redefined continuously. Second, the rate of access to college should not show pronounced discrepancies on common social indicators, for example, race, class, and so forth. Third, there is the implication of public responsibility to identify and alleviate barriers to universal access — how otherwise can generational inertia be overcome?

Currently, the problem of opportunity for higher education is discussed in several overlapping frames of reference. One is the question of minority representation and what must be done to solve the social problems related to it. Another is the role of selective institutions — more specifically, how they will select their students and how they will define their function. A third and more general question is how useful educational opportunity can be extended to a larger segment of high school graduates and the adult population.

A comparison may help to illustrate how these frames of reference differ. Throughout the country there are about 500 colleges selective enough to require a high school average of at least a B for admission (Willingham, 1970a). These colleges enroll almost 500,000 freshmen. If all these institutions were to admit a random group of high school graduates, they would presumably enroll 250,000 students who ranked in the bottom half of their high school class on any conventional measure of academic accomplishment. But there are now about 3.0 million high school graduates each year (United States Office of Education, 1968) or 1.5 million who rank in the bottom half. Even in this limiting case only one out of six bottom-half students could possibly attend one of these (formerly) selective institutions. Thus, the problem of educational opportunity is far broader than the important matter of appropriate representation of minority/poverty youth in the selective institution.

The point is not to understate either the current policy problems of selective institutions or the need to redress social imbalances, but to recognize these issues in the larger context. This paper is concerned with the broader interpretation of the problem primarily because it is difficult to discuss the relationship between opportunity and organization in any more narrow connection. Secondarily, information relevant to any of these problems is scarce, but it is possible to present some new data that bear upon the general matter of the accessibility of higher education and its organizational implications.

There are a number of exceedingly complex issues involved, and it should be obvious that the organization of higher education is only one aspect of those factors that influence individual opportunity in society. There is also the compelling influence of individual condition, social circumstance, and prior education. Furthermore, the ultimate issue is the distribution of privilege — probably less determined by education than by political power, economic realities, job opportunities, generalized racism, and various forms of social exploitation and bigotry.

From a completely different point of view, it is recognized that the development of real opportunity lies in the educational process of teaching and learning. The usable products of this process are confidence and competence, intellectual growth, and coping skill. Nonetheless access and certification are critical, and these plus the educational process are much dependent upon structures, planning, and policies; for example, organization. What are the major issues involved in organizing higher education for the purpose of expanding opportunity? The following paragraphs describe seven.

Major Issues

The functions of higher education. Much of the uncertainty and controversy concerning expanded postsecondary education stems from fundamental disagreement regarding the priorities and (limited) resources that are to be applied to different functions of higher education. Often disagreements are all the more ambiguous because the functions go unstated. Furthermore, the various functions that higher education does perform can be slanted toward either a traditional scholastic or an expanded societal interpretation.

It is beyond the scope of this paper to attempt to do justice to so broad an issue as the functions of higher education; it is nonetheless useful to provide a few examples. Table 1 lists six functions and gives an illustrative scholastic interpretation of each plus an indication of what might be added under a broader societal interpretation. The scholastic model is familiar enough, even if sketchily outlined. It represents a traditional way of viewing postsecondary education, though there are various rather different manifestations such as the small liberal arts college or the research oriented university.

The expanded societal model adds features that have two general characteristics: an orientation toward people and service, and the inclusion of a much broader spectrum of society. In general the expansion of educational opportunity is associated with the societal interpretation, and increasing enrollment tends to force higher education in this direction. The issue is what priority shall be applied to frequently divergent objectives such as those indicated in Table 1.

Universal access or universal attendance. A closely related issue is the proportion of the population that higher education attempts to serve directly. The Carnegie Commission (1970) makes a point of distinguishing universal access and universal attendance, saying:

"We do not believe that each young person should of necessity attend college. Quite the contrary. Many do not want and will not want to attend, and it cannot be shown that all young persons will benefit sufficiently from attendance to justify their time and the expense involved. . . We favor, on the other hand, universal access for those who want to enter institutions of higher education, are able to make reasonable progress after enrollment, and can benefit from attendance."

The distinction is valid and critical — regrettably, it is probably also incom-

Table 1. Illustrations of a Scholastic as Opposed to a Societal Interpretation of Various Functions of Higher Education

Functions of Higher Education	Objectives under a Scholastic Interpretation	Additional Objectives under a Societal Interpretation
Transmission of culture	Preserve the Western heritage	Enhance subculture identity
Individual development	Transmit middle-class morals and manners	Aid career development and social coping for most high school graduates and adults
Occupational training	Train professionals	Retrain and develop work-study ties at many occupational levels
Generation of knowledge	Develop the arts, sciences, and professions	Apply knowledge to social problems
Community service	Provide extension services (for example, agriculture and engineering)	Promote public service, support community action
Provide a national resource	Develop and maintain a specialized manpower pool	Absorb social pressure, for example, reintegration of servicemen, broaden social opportunity

patible with the Commission's "transcendent goal" of preventing the passing of inequality from generation to generation. It is increasingly recognized that large numbers of students both in and out of college simply have very little interest in the intellectual pursuits commonly reflected in higher education. The problem lies in the fact that many of these are the students who "inherit" unequal opportunity (Jaffe and Adams, 1969; Knoell, 1966). Therefore, efforts to equalize educational opportunity are frequently based on the assumption that higher education cannot lie passively in academic orthodoxy, but must add programs and living conditions that meet the needs and suit the life-styles of students who might otherwise find little reason to continue their education beyond high school. Thus, to minimize motivational and cultural barriers and to work effectively toward universal access to higher education is often to encourage universal attendance whether that is the intention or not.

The development of effective compromises between universal access and universal attendance is likely to be one of the more important and difficult problems in the organization of higher education over the next decade. One possible solution lies in the differentiation of institutions and programs. Another is the systematic development of attractive alternatives to college. But it is important to bear in mind that voluntary expression of different values and habits of various subcultures will surely result in different rates of college enrollment. Thus strict proportionate representation in higher education serves neither public nor individual interest, and who can easily tell when measures to insure universal access will, in fact, promote universal attendance?

There is here an obvious parallel to the development of compulsory attendance at the secondary level. Presumably we will never come to explicit attendance requirements at the college level, but certainly some of the problems generated by compulsory attendance in high school will find similar expression in high rates of college attendance. The parallel seems close enough to suggest the need for a detailed examination by thoughtful educators.

The content of higher education. The nature of the curriculum is obviously one of the critical issues in organizing higher education in order to expand opportunity. It is also far too complex to allow more than brief mention of a few general considerations. We start with the well-known fact that the content of higher education is now widely criticized on various grounds including an abstract discipline orientation, a lack of social involvement, inadequate personal relevance, and disinterest in the development of the student. (See Axelrod, et al., 1969; Katz, et al., 1968; Mayhew, 1969; Willingham, 1970b.)

Table 1 suggests that a rather different content is implied by a societal interpretation of higher education. New types of students not only require diverse subject matter but new styles, operating procedures, administrative arrangements, relationships with the surrounding community and the business world, and probably rather diverse working assumptions concerning the expected outcomes of the educational process. One would expect further diversity in the programs and institutions that are organized to serve different students and different needs under widely varying conditions. The problem is not merely to provide learning arrangements congenial to various minorities and subcultures; it is also necessary to maintain the functional integrity of the institution while insuring that there is real social and economic utility in the educational outcome.

The economic value of higher education has only recently been subjected to systematic analysis. Available data are typically crude, and many writers have commented upon the complex relationship between education and work. In a scholarly and dispassionate study, Becker (1964) concluded that even with ability controlled the rate of economic return to the average college entrant is substantial. In a less convincing but provocative analysis, Berg (1970) argues that the training value of education is oversold.

The highly regarded New Careers movement (Riessman and Popper, 1968) assumes that economic opportunity is inescapably linked to education but that radically new forms of organization are necessary in order to improve the training value of education and its direct connection to job opportunity. The basic idea of New Careers is to provide the undereducated poor with an immediate job in the framework of a career ladder, each step of which is associated with specific training and supplementary formal education. The model emphasizes community centered service careers.

These considerations suggest one organizational implication in particular. That is the desirability of extending opportunity through imbedding institutions in the culture, the commerce, and the unique life of the local community.

Local versus regional colleges. In the scholastic tradition, college is something you go away to. There are many well-known and obvious advantages to geographically centralized institutions of higher education. Concentration of resources facilitates efficiency. It also provides the critical mass necessary for academic scholarship. It is probably easier to add to existing colleges than to build new ones, particularly if the campus is located in a socially detached and esthetically pleasant environment. And there is the legitimate argument that the socialization of young adults is furthered by their leaving home at age 18. These considerations provide counterpoint to arguments favoring local institutions.

Perhaps the dominant consideration is money. Whether the local college is actually cheaper than regional higher education in the broadest possible sense of national economy is an uncertain point. But in the reality of current conditions and legislative habits, the local two-year college is an inexpensive way to extend educational opportunity. It is also relatively inexpensive for the student for a number of obvious reasons. Thus, the alternative of local colleges mostly supported by local taxes is particularly attractive in lean fiscal periods such as the present.

Under a societal interpretation of the functions of higher education, there are many additional considerations. One set of issues concerns the relationship between proximity and opportunity. In the case of many youth to whom equal opportunity would be directed, college is a foreign experience, distant with respect to culture as well as geography. It is becoming increasingly recognized that the strangeness of middle-class institutions and their uncertain practical relevance to immediate problems of marginal students are major barriers to higher education for the minority/poverty population (Knoell, 1970). It seems reasonable to assume that a local institution can reduce this psychological distance in ways that would be difficult or impossible for a regional college to accomplish. Added to these sociocultural advantages of the local college is the fact that the student can live at home, work part-time, and attend classes under circumstances which only commuting status permits.

There is some empirical evidence that these assumptions are valid. Several studies over the past 25 years have indicated that the attractive pull of a college dissipates rapidly with distance, and that the college access rate of local high school graduates is substantially higher in communities that have an inexpensive, nonselective college as compared with those that do not have such a college (see Willingham, 1970a).

Another set of issues stems from the expanding functions of higher education. Returning again to Table 1, the societal emphasis is upon such locally oriented objectives as enhancing subculture identity, direct work-study ties, continuing education, community action, and application of knowledge to real social problems. One can hardly say that such objectives are warmly and uniformly embraced by higher education; they reflect, however, the insurrection of youth, the expectations of the excluded, and very likely the necessities of the future. Again, the major challenge is to create an organizational structure which will compromise the choice between local and regional institutions and develop the complementary objectives and potential of each.

Autonomy versus control. If equal opportunity means that no segment of society be grossly and unreasonably underrepresented in higher education, and if these goals are other than mere words, then it seems very likely that coordinated public action is required. Kirp (1969) discusses equal educational opportunity as a corollary of recent constitutional interpretations involving criminal process and sufferage — both, like education, bearing upon fundamental individual rights due equal protection under the law. He quotes Fortas, saying:

"The significance of the [criminal process] cases in terms of our national philosophy, goes beyond the criminal law. Apart from their specific meaning . . . they stand for the proposition that *the state may be obligated in some situations to bridge the gap which indigency has created between a person and his constitutional rights.* They represent a refusal to accept the fact of poverty as relieving the state from an affirmative duty to assure that all persons have access to constitutional rights. They request the state to do whatever is necessary, even if it means spending state funds, to make constitutional rights a living reality for everyone."

Kirp goes on to argue that the state has a vastly greater responsibility regarding equality of educational opportunity than it presently accepts. From the foregoing considerations, this responsibility would certainly include monitoring the real conditions of educational opportunity, planning the means whereby opportunity is fostered, developing public support for necessary programs, and coordinating programs in the individual and public interest.

Statewide planning and coordination has developed markedly over the past decade (Mayhew, 1968; Palola, et al., 1970), as has the complementary technology represented by cost-benefit accounting procedures and management information systems (Western Interstate Commission on Higher Education, 1969). There is, however, the unpromising possibility that these developments are outrunning the social and educational philosophies they supposedly serve. For up to now relatively little attention has been given to such questions as: What types of data are necessary to monitor the protection of basic rights? What forms of coordination further what forms of opportunity? In what ways does state planning stifle or encourage local initiative?

A fundamental problem lies in the fact that a guarantee of equal opportunity requires central control and planning, but at the same time, effective opportunity seems very much dependent on the local initiative and commitment which autonomy allows. In the possibility of independent action lies the main incentive for institutions and their units to create relevant programs, to develop new entanglements with the business and cultural environment, and to put message ahead of medium.

Who will pay? It is clear enough that a substantial expansion and equalization of opportunity for higher education will cost a vast amount of money — money to support students unable to pay, money for additional facilities, and money for far more intensive programs at all age levels. This particular paper is not intended even to introduce the intricacies of financing higher education, but it must be at least recognized that the topic bears a decisive relationship to how higher education is organized and the opportunity it provides. Suffice it to ask three questions.

First, to what extent will higher education be supported by direct payment of student fees as opposed to indirect support of institutions? The former is assumed to put the burden where it belongs and to facilitate consumer satisfaction. Witnessing the commercial activities of some proprietary institutions leads some educators to question those assumptions. It is also argued, too often without convincing evidence, that educational opportunity in the public interest is best organized and planned rather than left to the vagaries of consumer demand.

Second, what sources of public support — local, state, and federal — will facilitate the most effective organization of higher education? It is generally presumed that the only large source of funds is federal revenue funneled through state agencies, yet this arrangement can further undermine indispensable community and institutional autonomy. How, for example, can higher education be so organized that a power elite in the state does not make decisions regarding allocation of resources to meet its own perception of need at the expense of powerless elements of society?

Third, how will aid be packaged nationally to students in different economic circumstances? The extent to which aid is made available as grants, loans, or work, and the conditions under which it is awarded may have as much bearing upon access to college as the availability of aid per se. From legislation to individual aid decisions, there are many opportunities for financial aid to miss those who need it most.

What access criteria? The issue of access criteria is mainly the question of who will have access to what institutions and programs? The question requires no introduction; this conference will doubtless elaborate it in some detail. There are, however, a number of vital national interests to be considered. For example:

— to create genuine opportunity for fulfillment of diverse individual interests and abilities
— to encourage diversity among institutions
— to maximize the utilization of high level talent
— to maintain the sorting and striving process that feeds aspiration and rewards accomplishment
— to maintain systems of evaluation and certification that are individually fair and socially useful
— to rectify serious imbalances in social opportunity

Many criteria determine the conditions of access to college. They include the personal and academic attributes of students, the policies and practices of institutions, the background characteristics that fix the course of secondary education and the student's motivation to continue, and such ancillary restraints as the cost of attending college and the lack of relevant programs where students need them. Naturally, these matters take on very different priorities depending upon what aspect of the total problem one is concerned with. For the remainder of this paper I shall focus upon some relatively simple institutional variables that permit estimates of the present degree of accessibility of higher education throughout the country. This discussion emphasizes system or state-wide organization. Special admission programs and open-door divisions of selective institutions represent ways in which access is being organized at the institutional level.

Accessibility of United States Colleges

The foregoing discussion of major issues elaborates the obvious conclusion that educational opportunity is connected in innumerable complex ways to the organization of higher education. A primary question is the extent to which colleges are now accessible and what populations they serve. The data to be reported are based on a demographic analysis of all 2,600 recognized colleges in the United States.[2] The basic question is how many and what sort of people live within commuting distance of an accessible institution. This is clearly a very incomplete view of educational opportunity, but the procedure provides national base line data that tell us something about the relationship between the organization of higher education and the issues that have been previously outlined.

In this study free-access higher education was defined to include three characteristics: It must be relatively inexpensive so that cost does not arbitrarily exclude those who cannot pay or are unwilling to burden an uncertain future with a long-term debt; it must be willing to admit the majority of high school graduates; and it must exist in such proximity that neither geographical nor psychological distance constitutes a major barrier.

In order to incorporate these three characteristics, each college in the country was rated on a five-point scale based jointly on tuition and selectivity. For the purposes of this analysis the two lowest levels were designated "free-access" colleges. Of some 2,600 colleges, 789 or about 3 in 10 were free-access as of fall 1968. In practical terms this means that they charged no more than $400 in annual tuition, and at least one-third of their freshman class ranked in the bottom half at high school graduation. This criterion of selectivity was chosen because a number of institutions are ostensibly open-door but de facto selective.

Of those colleges which were not free-access, 500 were excluded because they are special purpose or heavily religious colleges; the remaining 1,300 or so institutions were inaccessible in roughly equal measure because of cost or selectivity — but more often both. Free-access higher education, as here defined, is almost exclusively public. It constitutes 60 percent of the public and 1 percent of the private sector. Accessible higher education is also very heavily represented by two-year colleges that constitute three quarters of the total free-access group. Three out of 10 public senior institutions are free-access; the same proportion holds for their branches.

The 789 free-access colleges were plotted on detailed maps with commuting

---

2. A detailed report of this study including an analysis of the accessibility of higher education in each of the 50 states is available from the College Board under the title, *Free-access Higher Education.*

perimeters around each. On the basis of results of prior studies and various rules of thumb used by state planning agencies, a one-way commuting guideline or 45 minutes was used in this study. This time interval was translated into a commuting radius that ranged from 2½ miles in the largest cities to 25 miles in small towns or rural areas.

The national picture. It turns out that 42 percent of the population lives within these commuting areas. In a sense it is remarkable that the country has developed accessible higher education to this extent. On the other hand, educational opportunity for three-fifths of the population is inhibited by the simple fact that they do not happen to live near an accessible college. This is one of the less complicated indices of how far the country has to go in equalizing educational opportunity.

There are systematic differences in the proportion of people living near free-access colleges in different types of communities. As Table 2 shows, a small metropolitan area is the most favorable location for a poor, marginal student to find accessible higher education. It is largely unavoidable that students in sparsely populated areas are less likely to live near an accessible college.

Table 2. Percentage of Different Populations within Commuting Distance of a Free-Access College in the 50 States

		Total Percent within Commuting Distance			
Area	Population (millions)	White	Black	Mexican-American†	All U.S.
Metropolitan Areas (SMSA)*					
1,000,000+					
Central Cities	32.6	36	42	42	38
Fringe	33.2	37	31	68	37
500,000 to 1,000,000	20.0	36	46	66	38
250,000 to 500,000	16.0	47	61	37	48
50,000 to 250,000	16.2	62	70	56	63
Counties not in SMSA's					
Over 20,000	45.0	48	52	42	48
Under 20,000	16.2	24	27	13	24
All U.S.	179.3	42	47	47	42

* Standard Metropolitan Statistical Area
† Mexican-American in five Southwestern states; also includes Puerto Ricans in New York City and Chicago.

On the other hand, the orderly differences in accessibility among different-sized metropolitan areas make little sense. Metropolitan areas of one-half million or more appear frequently shortchanged when it comes to accessible higher education.

Of the 29 metropolitan areas that have a population of more than one million, Atlanta, Boston, Buffalo, Cincinnati, Detroit, and Paterson-Clifton-Passaic did not have one free-access college located within their city limits as of fall 1968. In 17 additional metropolitan areas, less than one-third of the central city or fringe population lives within commuting distance of a free-access college. Thus 23 of the 29 largest cities in the country have a major deficiency in the accessibility of higher education. Equally disturbing is the number of metropolitan areas that have no free-access college at all. As of 1968, the Census Bureau defined 228 Standard Metropolitan Statistical Areas, most of which had a population of 100,000 or greater. In 102 metropolitan areas the principal city has no free-access colleges.

Table 2 also indicates that blacks are somewhat more likely than whites to live near a free-access college in all types of communities except the fringes of the largest cities (where they are least numerous). Mexican Americans (in the five Southwestern states) and Puerto Ricans (in New York City and Chicago) are also somewhat more likely to live near an accessible college than are whites.

While it is also true that the overall analysis indicated no marked regional variations in the percentage of blacks living near free-access colleges, there are some very important exceptions and qualifications. First, there are states and metropolitan areas where these generalizations do not hold. In California, Maryland, Massachusetts, Nebraska, and New York, substantially fewer blacks than whites live near accessible institutions. The same is true in the metropolitan areas of Atlanta, Boston, Buffalo, and Los Angeles. On the other hand, there are states and metropolitan areas where blacks are much more likely than whites to live within commuting distance of a free-access college. The best statewide examples are Missouri, New Jersey, and Pennsylvania; a similar trend exists in the metropolitan areas of Kansas City, Milwaukee, and Newark.

Another general exception to the data on minority groups cited in Table 2 is the problem of discrimination. This is another form of selectivity that can make an institution inaccessible just as surely as cost or academic requirements. Through much of the country one must simply introduce a subjective "correction" for the obvious fact that much of higher education is, for many reasons, less accessible to blacks and other sociocultural minorities than to middle-class whites.

Regional variations. The accessibility of higher education varies markedly among the four main census regions of the country but not always in expected ways. The Northeast, for example, has never been a region known for accessible colleges. Private education has been dominant to such an extent that some states — particularly New York and more recently Pennsylvania — have purposefully allocated substantial student aid resources in order to use the private sector for public purposes. Furthermore, the Northeast has been slow to develop the egalitarian interpretations of higher education represented by the community college and comprehensive postsecondary educational opportunity.

Despite these facts the Northeast is only slightly below the national average with respect to the proportion of people living within commuting distance of a free-access college. As Table 3 indicates, this region falls behind the South and West only in metropolitan areas of one-half million or more people. However, such areas contain two-thirds of the population in the Northeast. In addition to its urban problem, the Northeast has frequently not developed and supported its free-access institutions; public higher education in the region often receives niggardly appropriations (*Chronicle of Higher Education,* 1969).

The Midwest is the surprise of the four regions. Its state institutions, long a source of national pride, have been identified historically with inexpensive, nonselective admissions. The data of Table 3 seem inconsistent with this tradition. The proportion of people living near an accessible college is substantially

Table 3. Percentage of the Population within Commuting Distance of a Free-Access College in Different Types of Communities for Each Region

Area	Northeast	Midwest	South	West
Metropolitan Areas (SMSA)				
1,000,000+				
Central Cities	29	44	38	44
Fringe	27	30	38	62
500,000 to 1,000,000	38	12	53	55
250,000 to 500,000	49	39	53	48
50,000 to 250,000	71	47	71	61
Counties not in SMSA's				
Over 20,000	51	35	55	50
Under 20,000	24	23	28	17
Overall percentage for each region	38	33	50	51

lower in the Midwest than in other regions. The largest cities appear better off than the Midwest generally; the principal reason is the existence of the community college systems of Chicago and St. Louis. These systems serve a great many people and seem attributable to unusual leadership. They are not typical of the region; of all moderately large metropolitan areas in the country without any free-access colleges, more than half are located in the Midwest.

It should be recognized that many state universities have nonselective colleges or divisions. Also, a number of public institutions are officially open to any high school graduate in the state but enroll most of their students from the top half of the high school class. Both these circumstances may be more common in the Midwest than in other regions. In neither case are such institutions classified here as free-access because the definition depends not upon whether *some* less apt students are admitted, but whether the total institution is likely to be regarded by prospective students as truly accessible. The best generally available measure of accessibility would seem to be the proportion of bottom-half high school graduates actually on the campus.

The situation in the South is interesting for several reasons. Despite very limited resources and a decentralized population, the region has managed to place free-access colleges within almost as large a proportion of its people as is true in the wealthier and more centralized West. This has come about through the use of widely different models. The comprehensive junior colleges of Florida, the technical education centers of South Carolina, the open-door senior institutions of Louisiana, and the university two-year system of Kentucky are good examples of this diversity.

Concerning the accessibility of higher education, the Southern region has two large problems — too well-known to belabor and too critical to dismiss. Racial segregation of institutions will necessarily hinder educational opportunity as long as it drains attention and resources from the development of relevant educational opportunity for high school graduates. And it is the limited resources and opportunities that constitute a second difficult problem. In spite of considerable progress in making higher education available to their youth, some Southern states still have a very low rate of college attendance.

Roughly half of the population in the Western United States lives near an accessible institution. This proportion is somehow lower than one might have expected, but it is important to recognize one other important characteristic of the West. Individual free-access colleges in this region are highly developed. They typically offer comprehensive programs, provide an array of community services, and attract large numbers of students. In this sense free-access higher education is particularly well developed in the West as compared to the Northeast. The extent of geographic variation is indicated by the percentage of new freshmen in each region enrolled in a free-access college: Northeast, 22 percent; Midwest, 34 percent; South, 50 percent; and West, 71 percent.

Organization and Opportunity

The nature and extent of interstate variations in accessibility are particularly important because this is the level at which public higher education is usually organized. To put it more explicitly, this is increasingly where broad policy is established concerning the type, location, and access characteristics of institutions. Considering that the general objectives of most states would presumably be fairly similar, there are remarkable differences in the scope of free-access higher education from state to state. In this section I will comment on the organizational character of those variations as they relate to the major issues outlined earlier.

The extent to which the population is covered by free-access colleges in individual states varies from 0 to 80 percent. In some states the accessible colleges are quite well situated in relation to the population; in others, where people live seems hardly to be a factor in the location of free-access colleges. The type of institution that serves the free-access function also varies a great deal across states. In some states free-access colleges are coordinated through a detailed plan; in some, organization is almost nonexistent. Finally, the states vary considerably with respect to the major problems they face in extending educational opportunity.[3]

Since attempts at statewide planning for educational opportunity are mostly rather new, it is improper to speak of state models of organization in any strict sense. There are, however, styles and approaches that characterize some states more than others. The four types of organization described below are concerned with the public sector because public institutions are subject to such organization, and they bear the public responsibility for educational opportunity beyond high school. In many states private colleges are included in state planning and coordination on a voluntary basis; obviously, the educational functions they serve in a state often have a pronounced effect upon allocation of state resources to public institutions.

---

3. As one would expect there has been considerable progress in the development of free-access higher education over the past decade. A detailed study nearing completion by Richard I. Ferrin of the College Board's Access Research Office indicates that the number of Americans living near a free-access college more than doubled between 1958 and 1968, but that half of that increase was eroded by other factors, principally the increasing selectivity of state colleges. A particularly valuable aspect of this study is the documentation it provides concerning the marked improvement in some states that have purposefully organized their systems of higher education to expand educational opportunity.

Differentiated organization. A differentiated form of state organization implies several types of institutions within a state, usually with little coordination among them. There are at least a dozen states that can be so characterized. They vary widely in the extent to which they provide accessible higher education. Examples include Wisconsin with its mixture of systems, Alabama with its numerous but somewhat uncoordinated junior colleges, and South Carolina with its extensive but partly unrecognized system of technical institutes.

While we are witnessing a marked increase in statewide coordination generally, this does not necessarily mean that fewer states will have a differentiated form of organization. It seems likely that some states will develop different parallel systems only loosely connected with one another. The recent extensive development of postsecondary vocational education outside the framework of higher education is the best current example (Swanson, 1968). This form of differentiation bears unfortunate resemblance to tracking in secondary schools.

A primary advantage of the differentiated form of higher education is the freedom it allows different types of institutions to develop their own strengths, without the in-fighting and status problems that can result when one institution serves multiple functions. Some major disadvantages affecting educational opportunity include inadequate local program alternatives for the student, difficulty in the development of coordinated guidance systems, and lack of flexibility in transferring among types of institutions. In some areas there is increasing social pressure against attending second-class (different) institutions. This may inhibit intentional development of specialized parallel systems.

This differentiated form of organization seems likely to spring up in a vacuum —either an interest vacuum or a power vacuum. There have been numerous examples of the former when new types of institutions have developed out of societal pressure and the indifference of existing colleges. Educational opportunity is extended over the short term but educational Balkanization may be the long term result. The power vacuum may be developing in some states where the statewide coordinating body lacks sufficient legal sanction to insure adequate coordination among parallel systems. For example, serious transfer problems in California suggest that that state has some of the symptoms if not the disease (*San Francisco Chronicle,* 1969).

Homogeneous organization. A homogeneous form of state organization characterizes some 8 to 10 states in which there is relatively little differentiation or coordination among institutions. In a sense we are dealing with a state of affairs as much as a model. In these states the diversified senior institution is the predominant type of college. They may be largely free-access like the state colleges of Arkansas, or moderately selective like the public institutions of

South Dakota. Indiana illustrates an important variation of this type of organization — the extension of senior institutions by means of branches. This represents an organized effort to extend opportunity through minimizing geographical barriers, but the access characteristics and programs of the branches are otherwise similar to those of the parent institution. A noteworthy finding was that most branches throughout the country were not free-access; I shall come to an important exception.

This homogeneous form of organization may ultimately encourage each institution to serve a broad range of scholastic and societal functions. But this would be an extremely costly development and there is some doubt that present undifferentiated senior institutions and their branches are likely to expand educational opportunity in the immediate future to the extent that other models can. In most of these states the colleges typically admit top-half students, and there are relatively few free-access institutions. Furthermore, this model gives limited attention to students not interested in traditional higher education.

Hierarchical organization. Without doubt the wave of the 1960s has been the California model. This hierarchical form of organization has three basic characteristics that bear upon educational opportunity. First, it is a differentiated multilevel system. Its community college base has a societal orientation with respect to access and programs. Its university top layer has a pronounced scholastic orientation. Second, there is a commitment to provide ready geographic access at low cost to as large a proportion of the population as possible. Third, the overall system is coordinated with respect to objectives, programs, transfer among units, and so forth.

Some 15 states have incorporated this general form of organization; an additional 10 or so are moving in this direction. Since a model is not easily imposed upon existing institutions, there are naturally many compromises and variations on the hierarchical form. Also, there are a number of conscious variations. One of the most important with respect to educational opportunity is the upper-division institution that receives all of its students as transfers from two-year colleges. This Florida experiment is being repeated in Illinois; both states are prominent in the development of the hierarchical model.

In its full expression the model is designed to integrate the societal and scholastic functions of higher education. For that reason it has highly significant built-in strengths — so many strengths in fact that it becomes particularly important to recognize its weaknesses. The community colleges have experienced serious difficulty in creating genuine opportunity for fulfillment of diverse interests and talents. This problem is evident in low enrollment in career programs and high attrition generally (Florida Research Council, 1969; Coordinating Council for Higher Education, 1969). Inadequate space for transfer students in senior institutions has become very serious in some areas and is likely to become more so (Willingham and Findikyan, 1969). And the model has yet to develop fully the community ties necessary to insure reliable financial support, provide extensive work-study relationships, and generate truly diverse institutions.

It seems inevitable that variations of the hierarchical model will continue to characterize emerging state plans. It is regrettable that part of this movement is due to the wrong reason — a not uncommon assumption that the community college is an inexpensive way to buy off large responsibilities. In truth the community college probably represents a farsighted wedding of ideology and practicality in the progressive move to a greatly improved but far more expensive form of community higher education.

Integrated organization. A final form of state organization closely related to the hierarchical model is the integrated system found in only three states — Alaska, Hawaii, and Kentucky (New York is a doubtful fourth). The important feature is the fact that comprehensive community colleges are organized as branches of the state university. This form of organization furthers societal objectives in a system which places priority upon governance, control, and integration of resources. But it may give up a good measure of the initiative and diversity that local autonomy implies.

This model is important because it represents a ready organizational alternative to the hierarchical plan. And it is an alternative which may be seized in response to social pressure on admission policy. For example, the City University of New York has developed what is probably the nation's most comprehensive master plan for urban education (Board of Higher Education, City University of New York, 1968). Its recent policy adjustments seem to have moved from a hierarchical toward an integrated model. This type of model also bears watching because it has the potential for improving upon the hierarchical plan or, in some states, perhaps moving in the other direction to a more orthodox system of university branches emphasizing scholastic functions.

A Final Impression

From a societal viewpoint the matter of educational opportunity is for many students a question of:

- whether there is a local college
- whether it is accessible
- whether it has relevant programs
- whether its programs lead to educational-vocational opportunities

With respect to the latter two points, there is ample reason for doubt and concern but inadequate facts. Concerning the first two points there is direct evidence of substantial deficiencies in accessible higher education throughout the country, serious inequities among cities and states, and harmful lack of coordinated planning in many states. These are basically problems of organization and resource development at the system, state, and national level. The job, for state planning bodies in particular, is to:

- collect systematic information in order to monitor access, inform the public, plan programs, and justify expenditures
- coordinate programs in order to broaden opportunity, reduce undesirable overlap, and insure educational relevance and continuity
- provide the forum and the leadership which will further social, fiscal, and educational responsibility in the public interest

I have referred to the state's legal responsibilities regarding educational opportunity. There seems little doubt that states have vastly greater social and educational responsibilities than they have yet accepted. With mounting costs and public involvement, it seems inevitable that there will be tremendous pressure to further organize the coordination and planning of higher education at the state level. It can be hoped there will be new models with improved characteristics and constructive alternatives to present limited forms of organization.

Many bridle at the whole message, feeling that the emphasis on societal objectives is doing great damage to higher education. This seems very likely true when such objectives are channeled into campus radicalism, precipitous reconstitution, and academic anti-intellectualism. It seems very doubtful, however, that there is any turning back from constructive movement toward expanded societal goals and greater efforts to serve larger numbers of youth and adults. A major problem is to enlist all available interest and talent in promoting societal objectives in ways that will preserve scholastic strengths.

During the sixties the country became committed to mass higher education. The seventies seem likely to be a critical period when second generation state planning and coordination will take hold and become entrenched in most states. It is hard to overstate the importance of this institutionalization of state organization. It is critical that it proceed in ways that will serve social ends but avoid bureaucratization, the stifling of institutional initiative, or constriction of individual choice. We seem certain to live with tension and compromise. In order to extend educational opportunity, it is vital that statewide planning work — but not too well.

References

Axelrod, Joseph; Freedman, Mervin B.; Hatch, Winslow R.; Katz, Joseph; and Sanford, Nevitt, *Search for Relevance.* San Francisco: Jossey-Bass, Inc., Publishers, 1969.

Becker, Gary S., *Human Capital.* New York: National Bureau of Economic Research, 1964.

Berg, Ivar, *Education and Jobs: The Great Training Robbery.* New York: Praeger Publishers, 1970.

Board of Higher Education in the City of New York, *Master Plan of the Board of Higher Education for the City University of New York.* New York: Coordinator of the Master Plan, City University of New York, 1968.

Carnegie Commission on Higher Education, *A Chance to Learn: An Action Agenda for Equal Opportunity in Higher Education.* New York: McGraw-Hill Book Company, 1970.

Chronicle of Higher Education, "What States Spend Per Capita, 1969." Vol. 4, No. 5, 1969c, p. 1.

Coleman, James S., "The Concept of Equality of Educational Opportunity." *Harvard Educational Review, Equal Educational Opportunity.* Cambridge: Harvard University Press, 1969.

Coordinating Council for Higher Education, *The Undergraduate Student and His Higher Education — Policies of California Colleges and Universities in the Next Decade.* Sacramento: Coordinating Council for Higher Education, 1969.

Educational Policies Commission, *Universal Opportunity for Education Beyond the High School.* Washington, D.C.: National Education Association, 1964.

Eisenhower Commission, *Goals for Americans: The Report of the President's Commission on National Goals.* Englewood Cliffs, N.J.: Prentice-Hall, 1960.

Ferrin, Richard I., *An Analysis of the Changes in Free-Access Higher Education in the United States from 1958–1968.* College Entrance Examination Board, Access Research Office, Palo Alto, Calif., in preparation.

Ferrin, Richard I., *Barriers to Universal Higher Education.* College Entrance Examination Board, Access Research Office, Palo Alto, Calif., 1970. Multilithed.

Florida Community Junior College Inter-Institutional Research Council, *A Follow-Up Study of First-Time-in-College Freshmen in Florida's Community Junior Colleges in Fall 1966.* Gainesville, Fla.: Institute of Higher Education, University of Florida, 1969.

Folger, John K., and Nam, Charles B., *Education of the American Population.* Washington, D.C.: U.S. Department of Commerce, Bureau of the Census, 1967.

Jaffe, Abram J., and Adams, Walter, *American Higher Education in Transition.* New York: Bureau of Applied Social Research, Columbia University, 1969.

Jencks, Christopher. "Social Stratification and Higher Education." *Harvard Educational Review,* Vol. 38, No. 2, pp. 277–316.

Katz, Joseph, and associates, *No Time for Youth.* San Francisco: Jossey-Bass, Inc., Publishers, 1968.

Kirp, David L., "The Poor, the Schools, and Equal Protection," in *Equal Educational Opportunity.* Cambridge: Harvard University Press, 1969.

Knoell, Dorothy M., *People Who Need College: A Report on Students We Have Yet to Serve.* Washington, D.C.: American Association of Junior Colleges, 1970.

Knoell, Dorothy M., *Toward Educational Opportunity for All.* Albany: State University of New York, 1966.

Mayhew, Lewis B., *Contemporary College Students and the Curriculum.* Research Monograph No. 14. Atlanta: Southern Regional Education Board, 1969.

Mayhew, Lewis B., *Long-Range Planning for Higher Education.* Washington, D.C.: National Institutes for Mental Health, Contract PH-43-66-1166, 1969.

Palola, Ernest G.; Lehmann, Timothy; Blischke, William R., *Statewide Planning in Higher Education.* Berkeley, Calif.: Center for Research and Development in Higher Education, University of California, 1969.

Reissman, Frank, and Popper, Hermine I., *Up from Poverty.* New York: Harper & Row, Publishers, 1968.

San Francisco Chronicle, State College Campuses Overflow. October 2, 1969, p.1.

Swanson, J. Chester, *Leadership Role, Functions, Procedures of Vocational-Technical Education Agencies at the State Level.* Vol. I. *A nationwide survey of status and organization 1966–67.* Berkeley, Calif.: University of California, 1968.

U.S. Bureau of the Census, *Estimates of the Population of the United States, by Age, Race, and Sex: July 1, 1967 to July 1, 1969.* Washington, D.C.: Government Printing Office, CPR, Series P-25, No. 441, 1970.

U.S. Office of Education, *Open Fall Enrollment.* Washington, D.C.: Government Printing Office, 1958 and 1968.

U.S. Office of Education, *Projections of Educational Statistics to 1977–78.* Washington, D.C.: U.S. Office of Education, 1969.

U.S. Office of Education, *Trends in Post-Secondary Education.* Washington, D.C.: Government Printing Office, (in press).

Western Interstate Commission on Higher Education, *Progress of the Management Information Systems Program.* Boulder, Colo.: Western Interstate Commission on Higher Education, 1969.

Willingham, Warren W., *Free-access Higher Education.* New York: College Entrance Examination Board, 1970, 240 pp.

Willingham, Warren W., "The Importance of Relevance in Expanding Post-Secondary Education." *Trends in Post-Secondary Education.* Washington, D.C.: Government Printing Office, in press.

Willingham, Warren W., and Findikyan, Nurhan, *Patterns of Admission for Transfer Students.* New York: College Entrance Examination Board, 1969.

Uses and Abuses of Scholastic Aptitude and Achievement Tests

By B. Alden Thresher

The topic I have been asked to discuss can be treated in either of two contrasting ways. Taken in its most narrow and literal sense, this group of tests can be looked at as "givens," and consideration given to the wisest use of them. In this approach, tests are the independent variable, established and relatively unchanging. Then the operative question is: how can we best use them? This would be a legitimate inquiry, and within limits, a useful one.

In such a context, it would be appropriate to rehearse the standard good advice that is regularly included in College Board literature. All concerned would be warned not to overestimate the precision of test scores (despite the embarrassing presence of that third digit). It would be made clear that tests measure only a limited, though important range of abilities, and that many qualities making for "success" in college lie beyond their reach. Genuine cognitive improvement would be distinguished from "practice effects" and errors of measurement. The probabilistic nature of the entire operation would be stressed. It would be made clear that the Scholastic Aptitude Test is not something one can prepare for in a short period of time, that test items need not be merely factual, but may call rather on reasoning abilities in relation to a particular field of study, and that other predictors besides tests should be taken into account in admissions decisions.

I do not intend to follow this plan. I propose rather to look at tests as only a single element in an exceedingly complex system regulating access to post-secondary education. All elements of this system constantly shift and readjust themselves in response to social and psychological forces. The problems faced by minority and poverty groups in relation to education can best be analyzed in this broad context, rather than by looking at tests as an isolated and relatively stable phenomenon. Tests, with all their drawbacks, are still a useful empirical device if too much is not expected of them. Just as it is futile to try to hone and sharpen the predictive power of tests beyond a very rough approximation, so it is futile in constituting an entering class to seek to push the selection of students to the stage of superselection, using tests or any other means. Marianne Moore has compressed the key question into a single line: "Why dissect destiny with instruments more highly specialized than components of destiny itself?" The destiny of any student will be determined by a variety of tidal currents, rough bumps, chance contacts, accidents, pushes, and boosts. Among these components of destiny, these gross and compelling effects, variations in test scores generally play a minor part. And whether a particular destiny is welcome or not, good or bad, is more a subjective matter of the individual's system of values, than a measurable effect against any quantitative criterion.

The processes by means of which nearly two million boys and girls distribute themselves annually among some 2,200 institutions of more or less higher learning constitute a system of immense complexity. The social syntax that regulates this process is more than a mechanism, and more than an organism, though it has some of the homeostatic properties of an organism. The only word there is to denote such a phenomenon is "system," a term that implies that its elements are interconnected in various ways. Some of these involve negative feedback, giving rise to a self-regulatory tendency. Some involve positive feedback that generates situations of instability. Some become visible to us as slow, long-range historical processes. Others give rise to sudden eruptive events in areas which long had remained tranquil as if to illustrate Santayana's ominous remark, "The universe is full of coiled springs."

This is too vast a canvas to paint in a brief paper. I shall attempt merely to suggest in a kind of thumbnail sketch some of the elements that seem to me relevant to the problem. In particular, I want to dwell on the necessity for change, innovation, and experiment in new directions. It is inevitable that any device, such as tests, which must be administered in a routinized manner and on a large scale, will fall into grooves that become highly resistant to change. All of us who are or have been involved with the use of tests on a large scale have been, I think, unconsciously defenders of the status quo, insufficiently alert to the many alternatives open to us. We have been blind to the needs and wants of students, and too easily persuaded that in adopting policies that serve the convenience of a college or university, we are also serving the students' interest and the public interest. We need to be more sensitive to the position of the test-taking student as the defendant in an adversary proceeding, the outcome of which may be quite contrary to his interest as he sees it. With the best intentions in the world, we fail to appreciate, as he does, the sensation of being an experimental animal strapped to a board.

The antitest revolt has been simmering now for a generation. Most of the criticisms of tests have been thoroughly aired and are well known to groups of educators such as this. I shall, therefore, not labor them here in detail. But I should like to call attention to some sociological aspects of testing, and to some assumptions in test and admissions procedures, which raise doubts about their appropriateness in solving the pressing current problem of access to education for minority and poverty groups. The critics of tests have, I think, tended to concentrate their fire too much on this single target — tests. What they should rather be questioning is a complex of college admissions practices in which tests form only a single element. These practices rest on a set of unquestioned or frozen assumptions which, though customarily taken for granted, deserve to be sharply questioned.

In using admissions tests, we have tended to assume (1) that existing educational practices (and marks) in college constitute an acceptable criterion for test validation; (2) that if some selection is good, more selection is better; (3) that college dropouts are necessarily a bad thing; (4) that prediction is the central purpose of tests; (5) that a college should assemble as many "good" students as possible; (6) that early "bloomers" are best; and (7) that distinguished performance on the part of alumni necessarily reflects credit on a college. In fact, every one of these propositions is open to considerable doubt and question, as I have tried to indicate elsewhere (Thresher, 1968).

There is real danger that the College Board, as a leading exponent and exemplar of the standardized test device may fall into a kind of automatic defensive attitude toward critics. It is a very human trait to identify oneself with a particular part of a system, or with the particular embodiment of a principle with which one has long been concerned. It is difficult to conceive of effective education without some process of educational assessment. It is with this broad principle that we need to be concerned. But there can be many ways of carrying out assessment besides the current, almost universal employment of psychometrically oriented, mass administered, multiple choice, normative, adversarial, secure, speeded, pencil-and-paper tests.

I will not venture into the broader question whether in fact effective education is possible without some form of assessment. It is conceivable that there may be a kind of indeterminacy principle at work, by which education can *either* be infused with vital energy, *or* be susceptible of precise measurement, but not both. Perhaps, in Wordsworth's phrase, "we murder to dissect." But in a meritocratic culture ruled by a philosophy of logical positivism and based on behavioristic assumptions, such possibilities are little explored. Some thoughtful educators have begun to lose interest in tests. As Elting Morison put it, testifying before the College Board's Commission on Tests, "we are in the process, it seems to me, of trying to test the results of something we do not understand. We may even do violence to the process itself. What we need to know is how the mind, surrounded by a field of emotion, works, rather than what is useful for students to learn.''

Tests as we know them have proved a useful device for nearly half a century, and have met an apparent need in one stage in this country's development. Yet it is ironic that what started out (in the early history of the College Board) to be a device for mitigating chaos in college entrance requirements has brought instead, rather inadvertently, a kind of box-score competitiveness not congenial to the life of the intellect. It had been quite sensibly supposed up to the end of the nineteenth century that a certain minimum competence in Latin, Greek, and mathematics was essential for any college entrant. A set of common examinations organized in 1901 defined and guaranteed this competence. The later developmental work on standardized tests carried on by Carl Brigham and others was aimed at the praiseworthy purpose of objectively implementing this guarantee. That this made possible large-scale mechanized methods came as a convenient by-product. What had scarcely been foreseen was the practical substitution of national norms of a quantitative kind for the simple, commonsense notion of competence. Here was one of the origins of what Edgar Z. Friedenberg calls the ''anthrodrome''—the substitution of a race-track mentality for the sense of community in college and university. His epithet suggests greyhounds chasing a mechanical rabbit—not a happy metaphor for a society of scholars.

The problem now is not simply the nature of the tests, but rather the general ambiance within which they function. The ways in which colleges utilize tests in their admissions processes, often work harm to the student in the sensitive aspects of his own self-confidence, sense of identity, and that energy of spirit without which the cognitive aspects of learning become shriveled and lifeless.

The use of tests to select individuals for college admission exposes the individual student to the full hazard inherent in the probabilistic nature of the enterprise. The research use of tests to guide educational policy, as for example in the Coleman Report, represents a more legitimate use of the test device. Even though the device is empirical and imperfect, it yields in this latter context a useful result. None of the probabilistic hazards affect the individual. The project explores statistically a broad educational hypothesis, and does not alter the destiny of any individual student. And because the project is pitched to the level of elementary, common learnings, the conformist tendency inherent in the test principle can be seen as a virtue.

The practices of testing constitute a prime example of the general sociological principle that a new technology, innocently devised to meet a need, may, because of its very convenience and utility, harden into an uncomfortably rigid mold that comes to constrain and limit the very people whose convenience it was designed to serve. The automobile is of course the prime example of a technical device that has proliferated because of its obvious utility. In so doing, it has not only disrupted living patterns and the design of cities, but it has developed secondary and tertiary ill effects such as collisions, air pollution, noise, and congestion, which at the outset seemed negligible. In much the same way the apparent utility and convenience of testing in the current mode brings serious consequences as this style becomes so widespread as to dominate curriculums and teaching methods, and to distort students' concepts of the structure of knowledge and of the nature of intellectual values. In the 70 years of College Board history, there has been a kind of schizophrenic alternation between the notion that tests should determine the nature of the curriculum, and the opposite notion that the curriculum should be free and untrammeled by the influence of tests.

The automobile, like the standardized test, took its origin from a simple technical innovation that came to fruition in Europe around the turn of the century. Both devices owe their luxuriant growth more to the American genius for mass production and marketing than to any notable originality exhibited in their development since they reached these shores. The automobile has been characterized as an engineering success but a scientific failure. Something of the same dichotomy of attributes is manifest in the standardized test. Granted the initial premises on which it is based, its development is a triumph of logical and mathematical perfection. But not enough is known about the learning process, the structure of knowledge, or the nature of cognition to support any confidence that the testing process yields more than a superficial, empirical body of data.

This is not necessarily a fatal objection to tests. They are not the first example of a device that, like the flight of the bumble bee, is practically useful though theoretically impossible. That useful invention of the economic statisticians, the cost-of-living index, is another typical example of such an invention.

The principle is simple. You take the average unit price of a large number of commodities, weighted according to their relative importance, and see how this average changes from month to month or year to year. But the weights keep changing, the definition of a commodity keeps changing, some commodities disappear from the market, new commodities appear. So the overall conclusion is inescapable — that an accurate index number of prices is theoretically impossible to construct. Yet these indices are in wide use, and economists find them indispensable, but they know they must not push their use too far, or expect too much of them.

In much the same way the psychometric basis of testing seems to erect a formidable structure of mathematical logic on a foundation of psychological assumptions that are of uncertain validity. The logic is irrefutable, but little is known about the underlying psychology. I am not convinced that we educators have got fully to the bottom of the philosophical question of what we are measuring. The optimistic phrase "work sample" conceals unguessed mysteries. A number of critics have pointed out that current tests measure, not what the student knows, but what he does *not* know. But since what each of us does not know is for practical purposes infinite in extent, testing practice presupposes a theory of cognition based on the assumption that there exists a limited, definable corpus of "knowledge." Even tests carefully designed to measure intellectual skills rather than factual knowledge (and the Board has increased the proportion of these) are subject to a similar limitation. They simply identify gaps in a structure of "knowledge" made up of facts, theories, habits, conventions, and systems of symbols, together with the skills needed to manipulate these. Many critics are disturbed at this situation, considering how much some students know and can do beyond the predetermined corpus of knowledge. One wonders how much of the corpus itself is really essential, seeing how much is being dropped out of it as well as added to it year by year, and how arbitrary much of the content is. Old curriculums quickly begin to look quaint and outmoded. Conversely, today's students readily adapt themselves to the world around them without the armament of "essential knowledge" held indispensable only a few years ago. A 20-item multiple choice test to qualify for a driver's license is an appropriate use of the testing device because the corpus of knowledge involved is limited and precise, and the subject is "how to do it." Beyond such training uses, and very elementary "common learnings," the concept looks increasingly dubious. The mystery goes deeper than simply delimiting the corpus of knowledge. It is a question of how the subject is organized in the mind, and this is influenced by cultural and linguistic factors.

No doubt the sampling of knowledge by means of questions will have to continue for some time. The pioneer work of Piaget was slow in gaining recognition in this country because the prevalent quantified behavioral psychology produced an inhospitable atmosphere for his closely observed, qualitative observations. Now that Bruner and others are working along similar lines, we may see the beginnings of a theory of cognition that can be the basis of a quite different approach to the basic problem of educational assessment. But for some time, we shall certainly be stuck with standard tests. The problem is how to make the best of an admittedly inadequate device.

We in education have already learned to cringe when people talk about "intelligence tests," or even about a "g" factor. One wonders whether a cultural anthropologist would not cringe even more at our easy use of the term "aptitude." He might marvel at our arrogance in assigning any normative or absolute value to the symbol systems of a particular culture and to its traditional habits of thought. This is not a fanciful idea, but a pressing practical problem. Large minority groups in our population have rich, well-established cultures of their own — cultures with a high survival value in coping with difficult environments. We have to ask ourselves whether it is not we in the academic world who are "culturally deprived." If higher education could and would reach inside these cultures and seek to understand them, there might be less arrogant insistence that others must come the *whole* way toward our particular "correct" habits of thought. Not only contemporary test theory, but contemporary higher learning in general leaves little scope for Mark Twain's insight that "we are all ignorant, but of different things." The official posture of the academic world is: "If anything's known, we know it, and what we don't know isn't knowledge."

The entire educational system has assumed that its built-in academic standards are "correct." It has ignored the influx into society of other and different cultural elements and has not been zealous to devise newer and better educational strategies. In a pluralistic society, these ethnocentric and academocentric assumptions need to be greatly modified. The testing movement, however, has accentuated them. It is certain that we need to know much more about the deep linkages between cognitive processes and the emotional life of the individual before we can use test scores with real confidence. The bedrock reliance of psychometry upon validity studies is put in doubt if the criterion against which validation is carried out is itself dubious. This would be the case if the criterion turns out to be merely formal, traditional, or arbitrary, or seems irrelevant to the student, or involves a circular reasoning process because it resembles the test itself.

So educators need to take seriously the increasing chorus of public criticism about tests and testing. It is true that part of the conflict represents power struggles about which groups shall control testing, rather than issues of educational principle. Some of the critics are intemperate and extreme; some are far from disinterested and have been accused of making a career of criticism; and some blame tests for abuses more properly traceable to the misuse of tests, and to a misunderstanding of their nature and purpose. Yet the question persists whether a device that can be so badly misused and so widely misunderstood is really as good as it ought to be. Two genuine merits can be attributed to tests. They sometimes identify able students who have been out of favor with teachers because of hostile attitude, unconventional behavior, or the kind of unresponsiveness that makes them invisible; and they do now and then identify and appreciate the self-taught student, instead of serving as barriers against the able but poorly schooled.

Whatever the future may bring, it is certain that we are stuck with the current type of tests for some time to come, if only in default of something demonstrably better as judged by conventional validity standards. So there is a need to review carefully any steps that might be taken within the existing tradition, and without any radical change of philosophy to improve the situation of the student. I will mention three steps, though there is no time to elaborate them here.

First, I think it can be shown that current test practices give more weight to speed than is desirable. Second, much more could be done to make tests a student-centered device. If it is granted that normed tests, with all their drawbacks, still have a certain practical utility, the student himself can be made the primary client, not only reporting scores to him, but also making self-scored and self-administered tests available, and so letting him feel that the test is a service he himself buys in order to "take his own temperature." Along with this would go a broad effort to make available to him some discussion of the relative merits of various answers to a given item, in contrast to the insistence on one "right" answer. In the current adversarial mode of testing, the student reads the message, "They are more interested in appraising me than in educating me."

Third, more could be done with numerous tests of limited modules of subject matter up to an acceptable, absolute competence standard, without any effort at comparing this student with others. This would allow a college either to permit or to require a more flexible assortment of talents and achievements to be offered and sampled in connection with admissions decisions.

It is commonplace that admissions tests place too much emphasis on general academic ability, as judged by one or two major dimensions, and not enough to other talents. Furthermore, test results may set up a self-fulfilling prophecy; those students who do well in the aptitude tests also do well in the curriculum that is geared to the same habits of thought with which the tests concern themselves. It is common knowledge that there is a very uncertain relation between college grades and later social effectiveness in occupations other than specialized professional and scientific areas. If the curriculum itself is only partially relevant to the student's interests and objectives, and therefore provides a criterion of questionable value for test validation and for the screening and selection of students, the resulting meritocracy becomes diverted from rational human purpose.

To recognize adequately the interest of the individual will, however, require more than a change in tests. It will require a change in the habits and assumptions on which college admissions policy is based. When testing is focused primarily on the individual as client, rather than on the convenience of the college, there is imposed on colleges a greater obligation to take risks. Attrition is to be expected rather than shunned. If no attrition occurs, the college is playing it too safe. College dropouts are by no means always or necessarily a bad thing. The unexamined assumption that the version of educational experience that a particular faculty has generated (or imitated) is a valid educational standard results in many students being tagged as "failures" simply because they do not respond to that particular pattern of stimuli. A much freer movement of students among colleges is needed, nor should a student who has not done well in one place be treated as a leper, forever debarred from trying a different environment.

The court of last resort in the psychometric approach to testing is validity. Normative testing has led to a series of closed feedback loops through the following steps: (1) validation of tests (often combined with other predictors) against college performance as expressed, for example, in grade-point averages; (2) prediction of probable performance based on a regression formula derived from this validation; and (3) selection of entering students according to the formula, thus maximizing correlation between predictor and criterion. This is a tightly constrained system of reasoning that scarcely contemplates the possibility of any change in conventional faculty-oriented methods of presentation or of assessment. Now that something of a revolution in teaching methods is in progress, the reliance on validity as the bedrock foundation in testing is called in question. The uncomfortable possibility appears that some of the most vital and effective devices to stimulate learning do not lend themselves to quantitative assessment in ways such as we are accustomed to using.

The extraordinary contributions to society made by many college dropouts cast serious doubt on the conventional sequence of validation, prediction, and selection. Faculties tend to want the "best" students according to their own quite narrow criteria. There results a "collegiocentric" selection in which faculty preference and convenience often takes precedence over the student's interest in his own long-range development and social effectiveness. The unregenerate professor who remains untouched by any vision about the broad social consequences of education is happiest when he can teach more and more to fewer and fewer and better and better students. Faculty opinion is the dominant force in the admissions practices of the stronger institutions. The naive faculty view is: identify and exclude all candidates likely to do poorly. Then everyone will do well. This simplistic reasoning leaves out of account the probabilistic nature of all selection. To eliminate all the poor risks, you must also eliminate many good ones. The survivors, duly enrolled, proceed to distribute themselves all the way from the top to the bottom of the class, in accordance with the habit of faculties of raising their "standards" (that is, failing the same proportion) as fast as the classes improve. Much to their surprise, they find that every class has a bottom third, and that half their students are still below average in performance. This process goes on indefinitely, no matter how highly selected the class may be. So the deep roots of inertia reach back into the colleges and into beliefs about student selection that prove ill-founded. There is a real question (1) whether individual colleges *can* select the students who in the broadest sense are the most promising, or (2) whether colleges are, in the public interest, necessarily entitled to do so. Yet these two assumptions have been, from time immemorial, unquestioned dogma in most colleges.

The "faculty syndrome" includes these beliefs, often implicit rather than articulated: "Few if any students are adequately prepared. Since I must teach them from the ground up, I am entitled to have only the very best students, hence admission should be highly selective." The unconscious arrogance in this attitude is indeed an innocent arrogance, for it is deeply involved with the college teacher's intellectual integrity. These teachers are predominantly men of sensitive conscience and honorable intent. Yet the admixture of pedantry that any good teacher must have can render their judgments unduly rigid. And the pressure for admission to college sends a signal to the faculty mind: "We must be pretty good, since we are in such great demand."

Skepticism about the closed circle of validation, prediction, and selection is justified not only on these broad grounds but also more narrowly by increasing doubts about the entire structure of marks and grade-point averages in higher education. These expedients are being increasingly condemned as anti-intellectual in tendency.

A device that began as a practical convenience in dealing with large classes becomes an end in itself, diverting the attention of both teacher and student from the central concerns of intellectual development. In response to these doubts, the conventional structure of marks and course credits is being rapidly eroded by variants of pass-fail, as well as by more imaginative experiments. Not only are marks coming to be seen as minimum information devices; their use as a criterion is also open to question on the practical ground that they will be less available as time goes on, as well as less closely coupled with the realities of what is happening in the mind and heart of the student.

The conventional quantitative approach to testing emphasizes the status achieved after learning rather than an understanding of the process and mechanism by which learning occurs. Testing, if it is to represent assessment in the broadest terms, should determine the appropriate *complementation* rather than comparison. The student should be guided and educated to complement and extend the learning he already has, rather than just to compare it with the learning others have. Monitoring of performance as a basis for determining quality can best be an on-going part of teaching rather than primarily a means of determining the destiny of the individual. There is a wide field still undeveloped for the characterization (not necessarily measurement) of attitude, function, motivation, style, and temperament as well as of ability and achievement, and ample scope for research in developing the kinds of instruments needed for such characterization.

Prediction and selection can never be wholly eliminated in education, but increasing emphasis should be laid rather on diagnosis of the individual's needs and on prescribing the next step he should undertake. Testing with this objective would exist in an affirmative context of optimizing the benefits of the next step rather than in an exclusionary context of deciding who is to be denied a specified educational opportunity.

Above and beyond the parochial interests of the individual college, testing is closely related to the wider issue of whether the annual distribution of entering students among some 2,200 colleges approaches an optimum pattern from the standpoint of the public interest. No one knows whether it does, or whether it is possible to define or characterize such an optimum pattern of distribution. Few individual colleges have even glimpsed the existence of this issue, so intent are they on their own supposed institutional interests, and on the *bellum omnium contra omnes* which prevails in the world of college recruiting. The biologist, J. T. Bonner (1962), makes the arresting suggestion that the so-called selective colleges may in fact be all unconsciously effecting a kind of counterselection that diverts the most promising students into the nonselective and open-door colleges. Such recent studies as those by Alexander Astin (1962) and Dean Whitla (1968) are now for the first time opening up the possibility of studying this vital issue in a perspective as broad as the public interest.

The traditional approaches to testing for college admissions are ill-adapted to the diagnostic objective. They are essential only if one grants as valid current college faculty preferences and habits and current admissions policies centered on the supposed interests of particular institutions in maintaining these preferences and habits. These are in part traditional and retained through sheer inertia, but in large part they are traceable to the predilection of college teachers for those who are easiest and most fun to teach. These generally turn out to be those already furthest along toward becoming copies of the teacher himself. It is these students, in the jargon of the trade, who are said to be able to ''profit'' by higher education and the college admissions policy reflects the college's emphasis on attracting them. Humphrey Doermann's (1968) searching study of college competition to enroll ''the bright and the prosperous'' focuses attention on the ''collegiocentric'' posture of all college admissions.

Aptitude tests that measure mastery of the mother tongue of the dominant subculture impose a heavy and permanent handicap on most ethnic minority groups. There is a bitter truth in the oft-repeated injunction that one "cannot study for" the College Board's Scholastic Aptitude Test (SAT). One has to be born and raised to it. It is significant that "disadvantaged" students generally show a smaller lag in mathematical skills than in verbal skills; the quantitative symbol system is learned later and somewhat more artificially than the verbal system of the mother tongue. To learn it requires a conscious effort on the part of all, whether or not they are already at home in the use of the mother tongue. Thus, in arithmetic, all start more nearly even than in the use of standard English.

This issue about the "unfairness" of aptitude tests with reference to particular minority groups is of course an old one. The conclusions of most discussions about it are (1) that since competence in standard English is indeed a prerequisite to any effective higher education, aptitude tests, however "unfair," must continue to stand, and (2) that the remedy lies in early education, for example, Head Start and other programs. All this, up to a point, is true.

But there may be a broader dimension to the problem. To anyone brought up in traditional academic disciplines the written expression of many high school students, even those in the mainstream of the national culture, seems semiliterate and barbarous. Yet it is known that it is possible to function successfully and effectively in many useful roles in our society using language of a kind to make any college professor shudder. So the conjecture must be entertained that there may be a cultural lag here that will never be wholly made up. Standard English, SAT version, may be an echo from the past of a generation or two back. If (as seems to be the case) the effective work of the world in the long run turns out to be carried on in large measure by people with a very wide range of test scores and widely varying degrees of literacy, it may be that prim insistence on these so-called predictors is not so much a necessity as an academic foible.

There is a necessary tension between the formal, official, and literary language of any culture and the rude vigor of popular usage. Nearly all the new usages that spring from the vernacular and in due course find their way, over the centuries, into standard English, go through a period of being deplored by purists. Grace and precision in the use of language must continue to be a leading objective of education, but we should not debar from educational opportunity those who have not inherited these as a birthright.

The problems of minority- and poverty-group students need to be viewed constantly in broad perspective, educational and sociological. Theirs are, in fact, the same problems that bedevil all education, but intensified by the special disabilities that weigh them down. Our greatest potential asset is human diversity, our greatest failure our inability to develop and utilize it for the common good. As Emile Duclaux once said, "Nature loves diversity; education aims at repressing it." This in a nutshell is our dilemma. The pressure toward conformity that generates the intense conservatism of most education arises out of a dual necessity. It is essential to pass on to the student the culture into which he was born and of which, indeed, he was a member even before he was born. The binomial theorem, the Gettysburg Address, and numberless other legacies without which he would be helpless, need to be not only passed on to him, but in some fashion re-created in his own mind before he can possess them. Even more important than this substantive content of a culture is the language code by which he communicates with and understands his fellows. This, being complex and subtle, is best learned so early that its mastery lies below the level of conscious effort. So here are two massive necessities making for educational uniformity. How in the face of these can we urge, or even tolerate diversity? Simply because what we know and have achieved is only an infinitesimal fraction of what is possible. The universe, as has been well said, is not only stranger than we imagine, it is stranger than we *can* imagine. The potentialities of human diversity are boundless, yet the cement of custom, tradition, and habit are needed to keep society from flying apart. Such is our dilemma.

These are platitudes. What is their significance in the practical task of college admissions? I think that this line of thought casts serious doubt on the conventional assumptions underlying admission to higher education as hitherto practiced. The ignorant purposefulness of conventional admissions policy has been acceptable only because for the most part it went wide of its mark and so left scope for the random processes of nature to restore some of the balance that human obtuseness would upset. The typical admissions committee member, "most ignorant of what he's most assured," could do only a limited amount of damage because he could attain his objectives only imperfectly.

Educators have learned to identify, after a fashion, certain kinds of intellectual excellence, and these talents are indeed of vital importance. But these represent only a small part of the wide spectrum of human talent. We do not begin to understand the relation of testable knowledge to the immense diversity of human faculties which, as "moderator variables," constantly give rise to performance and achievement of the most unsuspected kinds. In particular, we do less than justice to the action-prone types, the doers, who find passive, discipline-oriented learning irksome. These types often respond with explosive energy and achievement to project- and problem-oriented study. We have barely made a start in bringing out the latent powers of such students. A discipline-oriented faculty finds it difficult to recast its thinking so as to reach these people. This is not to devalue learning. It is rather to bring the civilizing and intensifying effects of learning to bear on the energetic people who do most of the practical work of the world — in Stevenson's phrase those "who with laughter, song and shout, spin the great wheel of earth about."

We have learned up to a point, to identify and encourage the precocious — this has been done, to a limited extent, for centuries, thus opening up an important source of talent — even of genius. But the late bloomer is an equally important and much more neglected phenomenon. Whether because he blooms late or in spite of it (it is not known which), he may retain longer, in Bonner's hypothesis, plasticity, originality, and the power to go on learning together with the appetite for it. The Darwinian mind that can brood for a lifetime over a vast complexity of evidence is not well served by conventional college admissions methods. Neither is the mind that expends its energy in action forms, and is impatient of the systematic pedantry of plodding academics; or the chessmaster mind with its special, combative virtuosity.

To get away from the mindless, meritocratic treadmill of marks and test scores, some colleges have resorted to the "composed" class. They look for people who are "interesting" or who have evidenced special initiative or talent, perhaps in some unusual direction. This is good, up to a point. But it is predicated on the assumption that students are classifiable into simple, recognizable types — "the jock," "the reasonable adventurer," "the politician," "the tools," and so on. It is likely to overlook types of excellence not in the main stream of the value system of our era. And it is all predicated, too, on the assumption that the college must at all costs make the best possible showing in the crop of graduates it turns out. This unexamined assumption, which has attained the status of dogma, has two flaws.

First, it is assumed that a college can properly take credit for the performance of its alumni, a highly questionable belief. There is a good deal of evidence to show that the output of a college depends in large measure on the input (Astin, 1962). We need a measure analogous to what the United States Bureau of the Census calls "value added by manufacture." We might well find some colleges whose influence subtracts from the distinction of their graduates. Second, the true measure of a college's quality should properly appear from what it can do with a reasonably average cross section of intelligent youngsters. If it gives itself all the breaks in advance by picking students so able that nothing the faculty does to them will hurt them very much, we can't really say how good the college is. If a basketball coach takes only seven-footers, and wins all his games, we don't really know whether he is a good coach or not.

What is needed is to get away from the convention of talking about the "top" or "bottom" of a class, the "highest fifth" and all the rest of it. This jargon conceals the very diversity that is the life blood of education. This practice cannot be blamed on tests, since it is imbedded deep in the history of education. Phrases like "head boy" and "foot of the class" are ancient conventions, arising out of the conformist view of education. Tests have merely accentuated them.

In the days when college attendance was the special preserve of a small elite, superselection, though never a very practical goal, was at least a rational one. With more than half of high school graduates in some form of higher education, a scramble for outstanding students begins to look silly. It is not known how much damage is done by segregating in one institution a large group characterized by very high verbal and quantitative intelligence. Very possibly these people, in the public interest, ought to be spread thinner where they can serve as a focus of stimulation and illumination for their more pedestrian confreres. Certainly their own experience of the world and of humanity would be broader if their day-to-day associations in these formative years covered as broad a spectrum as possible of human types. They should not listen only to each other. In A. N. Whitehead's view, "pure intellect can easily become trivial in its grasp of reality." The scientist needs constantly to check deductive logic against the hard realities of experiment and observation. The fluent intellectual, all on fire with his interest in "ideas," needs to rub against his more stolid and taciturn brothers who provide the ballast in human affairs.

But, it will be objected, what if they cannot keep the pace, what if they are unprepared, what if they do not meet faculty standards? Obviously some floor has to be put under the entire operation. Realistically, it would be a slaughter to throw an unprepared student into a saber-toothed curriculum. The answer, I believe, is to do the very thing that conventional wisdom has usually advised against — set a cutoff point; but make it low. Temper the wind to the shorn lamb. Of course, all necessary help, counseling, encouragement, extra time, and remedial work needed must be provided. Accept some attrition. But put a humane floor under the entire operation. At the other end of the scale, those of exceptional precocity must of course be given a place. This leaves a considerable middle range — how wide would depend on the nature of the institution — where selective recruiting, on meritocratic principles though perhaps tempting from the college's viewpoint, is not in the public interest. Fill these places by random choice, perhaps in order of application, or some other arbitrary manner. This introduces a healthy diversity of human types which in the long run will yield wholly unpredictable combinations of talent. Above all, make every effort to hold on to the offbeat people so likely to be automatically refused admission under the conventional and received values of our society. It stands to reason that a selective process limited and hedged round by a particular value structure will miss many unrecognized sources of talent — hence White-head's view that only certain kinds of excellence are possible in particular historical eras. Meritocratic selection gets bound by its own inner logic to a particular range of criteria, and hence to a culture warped in particular directions. What I have just outlined offers, I believe, both the justification for a greater degree of "open admissions" and a rational basis for keeping it within realistic limits. But, it will be objected, selection is necessary in all branches of human endeavor — one does not choose a mate or hire a worker for any job without careful attention to selection — to fitting the person to the task. Is not selection even more important for education? The answer is, in principle, that everybody needs more education, and if he wants it, ought to get it. There may be room for argument over the particular stage and kind for which he is ready. But there is no such thing as an unfit or unqualified seeker after education. He may be unready for a particular institution, department, or stage of advancement, but there should be no such thing as refusal of educational opportunity.

It is my view that the divine right of any college to super-select to the utmost limit made possible by its reputation and drawing power is unwarranted arrogation of privilege. This must be tempered by a readiness to help the students near at hand who make up its natural clientele. "Open admission" is a dramatic phrase to call attention to this neglected truth.

I commend to your special attention Astin's brief article *Folklore of Selectivity* (1969), which cuts through a half century of sophistry on the subject of college admissions. He gives hard data to show that though disadvantaged minorities do make *lower marks* in college, their *dropout rate* is only slightly higher than that of typical students. If picking winners is a legitimate objective of admissions selection, meritocratic competition is a legitimate method. But if the object is to change the student, to optimize not marks, but the great task of human salvage, educators should seek out those most in need of education, not those already three parts educated. It is as if a hospital were to select only those patients easiest to cure, instead of those in most urgent need.

So we should hope to see in the years ahead a new equilibrium of forces and a new set of criteria for the distribution of students among colleges. Admissions, if not wholly "open," will be at least far less arbitrarily closed than before. Colleges and universities, far from suffering a breakdown of standards, can gain in breadth, compassion, and understanding of the true ends of intellectual endeavor. The intellectual arrogance that is the product of thinking in a closed subculture can give way to a tradition more deeply humanistic because it is more open, more tolerant, and in its catholicity more representative of the full range of human potentialities.

References

Astin, A. W., "The Folklore of Selectivity." *Saturday Review,* December 20, 1969.

Astin, A. W., "Productivity of Undergraduate Institutions." *Science,* April 13, 1962.

Bonner, J. T., "A Biologist Looks at Unnatural Selection." *Princeton Alumni Weekly,* November 23, 1962, pp. 6–16.

Doermann, Humphrey, *Crosscurrents in College Admissions.* New York: Teachers College Press, 1968.

Thresher, B. Alden, "Frozen Assumptions in Admissions," pp. 9–22 in *College Admissions Policies for the 1970s.* New York: College Entrance Examination Board, 1968.

Whitla, Dean K., "Candidate Overlap Studies and Other Admissions Research," pp. 137–165 in *College Admissions Policies for the 1970s.* New York: College Entrance Examination Board, 1968.

Response to B. Alden Thresher's Paper

By Alexander W. Astin

It is a rare experience to read a dissertation on a topic as close to my own interests as this one, and to find that I agree on so many basic points. Mr. Thresher's paper, in addition to being well-reasoned and erudite, is lively and a very real pleasure to read.

Perhaps the most relevant point among the many Mr. Thresher makes so well is his analogy to the automobile. It seems to me that we have become so mesmerized by the technology of tests that we have lost sight of the basic reasons for their use. In the familiar terminology of Gordon Allport, tests have become "functionally autonomous."

This phenomenon is well illustrated in the way test scores are computed. Rather than simply reporting raw scores to show how much a student knows about a particular topic, we instead compute percentiles, standard scores, and other derived scores that show only how he performs *relative* to others. While such scores may have certain desirable statistical properties, they are of little value in showing how much *learning* has taken place over time.

Perhaps the major reason for the heavy reliance on derived rather than raw scores is the fact that most of the tests taken by high school students are typically used for selection and placement rather than as measures of performance. Knowing how a person ranks relative to his peers greatly simplifies the problem of selection, as long as the purpose of the selection is simply to find the best performers. But is this really the most appropriate mission for college admissions officers? Is it simply a matter of finding the smartest, most accomplished, most able students? Do not colleges also have some responsibility to *educate* the student? It would seem that college admissions officers have adopted a meritocratic selection process that would be more appropriate for use in business and industry (where such competition for talent is necessary to maximize profits in a competitive environment) rather than for education, where the emphasis is presumably more on what the institution does for the student than on what the student does for the institution.

Of the three major proposals for change that Mr. Thresher makes, two implicitly involve a move from relative to absolute standards of performance. Mr. Thresher makes the point (and I think testing organizations are slowly coming around to the same view) that the possibility of using objective measurement to enhance the learning process—to give the student "knowledge of results" of his educational efforts—has never really been tried. As I have already suggested, absolute rather than relative measures of performance would seem to be more suited to this kind of application.

Mr. Thresher also makes the point, frequently overlooked by the purveyors of tests, that one cannot take refuge in the argument about the "predictive validity" of tests unless he can also justify the *criterion* against which the validity of the tests is evaluated. The college grade-point average has, of course, come under attack from many quarters. But even if one accepts college grades as valid measures of something important, is it enough simply to know that a particular test *predicts* grades? Does this mean that the "value added," in terms of the student's intellectual development, will be less for students who have low predicted grade-point averages than for those who have high predicted grade-point averages? Not at all. Again, we are faced here with the question of whether colleges are simply "picking winners" for later achievement or whether they are attempting to make a difference in how their students turn out. In this regard, Mr. Thresher notes that overemphasizing the strictly predictive approach may blind us to the educational processes that affect student learning and cognitive development.

Implicit in much of Mr. Thresher's challenges to our current admissions practices is a serious questioning of the higher educational system as it is currently structured. If I read him correctly, he is suggesting that the de facto track system that has evolved from competition for bright students may not be the most efficacious way to organize institutions of higher education. He suggests here that depriving many institutions of substantial numbers of the brightest and the most motivated students by concentrating them in a few institutions may have detrimental consequences for both types of institution. He suggests, further, that we may need a "diversity" that is more horizontal than vertical, in which the most talented people are more evenly distributed among the various units within the system.

From the point of view of the goals of this conference, the question remains as to how the giant testing organizations can get their efforts redirected. What is the mechanism for change? How do Mr. Thresher's ideas get translated into changes in educational practice? To use George Hanford's terminology, where is the "leverage" for implementing change?

One first step would be for most of us to acknowledge that the whole concept of selective admissions, as currently practiced by most colleges and supported by testing organizations, may be ill-conceived. Colleges are not businesses competing for a finite supply of talent. Admissions officers are not race-track handicappers who are simply trying to pick winners. Colleges should not simply select only those students who already know what the college is supposed to teach them. A vertical diversity of institutions based on segregation of students by ability is not necessarily the best system in terms of total educational benefit to the greatest number of students. The current use of massive national testing programs simply serves to support this type of stratification.

One barrier to change is that many prospective college students, parents, counselors, and others are handicapped by a lack of information. The testing organizations need to encourage colleges to make available much more comprehensive and usable data for college guidance. If selective admissions is to be abandoned and freedom of choice greatly increased, then such information is vital to assist students in making appropriate choices.

Perhaps the biggest threat to the testing organizations is the possibility that tests will lose their credibility over the long run and eventually be abandoned altogether. As long as testing organizations continue to give major emphasis to the meritocratic use of their tests in admissions, this unfortunate demise of the organizations remains as a real possibility. But such an eventuality would be a tragedy in the long run, since we *need* measurement in education. Students need to know what they have learned beyond the subjective judgments of their teachers, and teachers have a need to know, in some objective way, how their students are progressing. Educational planners and researchers need to know what students know and what they don't know in order to design appropriate educational environments and experiences. To put it in Mr. Thresher's terminology, more and better measurement is needed, but it should be less ''judgmental'' and more ''informative.''

Open Admissions:
Status, Trends, and Implications

By Timothy S. Healy

One of the classic regrets to which the well-bred denizens of America's private universities are given is the one provoked by the "political control" under which the public universities are said to operate. The assault on the California state system of higher education is the usual example given, but the clear implication is that what is true on the shores of the Pacific can be applied almost univocally to all public higher education. The image is evoked of the university president, standing hat in hand in the legislative anterooms bartering the intangibles of freedom and integrity for the hard cash needed to keep his classrooms heated, lighted, and, above all, filled. It is indeed an image calculated to fill the eye with tears, but there are several equivocations which it conceals. Some of them are minor — such as the simple fact that the private colleges in states like New York are also hanging decoratively around the same anterooms with, if one follows the image, much the same goods to offer in trade. As a matter of hard fact, they do rather more than hang about, since one of their major exercises has to be a delicate process of mutual throat-cutting, urban against rural, little against large, sectarian against nonsectarian.

There is, however, one major falsehood the beggar's image hides, and it is very much worth considering. As a matter of fact, there might now be ground for urging that in its relation to legislatures and other policy makers the public university is not following but leading. When the university is truly open, it contains among its thousands of faculty members and students, representatives of every economic level, of every racial and religious stream. It deals both abstractly and in its living with every tension and struggle that the city contains. It is in short a summary of its parent society. As such, it may well send its president off to barter with a pack of trade goods that do not include his honor but might carry the answers to many of the problems that bedevil the keepers of the public purse.

There is more than a little evidence that this is what is happening currently in New York. In this bifurcated state, half of which is one great city and the other half of which, like God, can define itself only in terms of negatives, most of the forces that threaten the present and will shape the future are brought to bear on The City University of New York long before they are shipped up-river to the rural peace of Albany.

It is often stated that the students attack the university since it is clearly the most vulnerable branch of the establishment — which is correct, no matter what one thinks of the aims or the methods of the attacks. There are, however, good grounds for making a further assumption. That is that the public university is the establishment's most forward foot. In hard demagogic terms, the revolutionaries' boast might be "give me a university as fulcrum and I will shift the establishment."

The City University of New York is a good example. With its 18 colleges and two graduate centers it can serve as the paradigm of the large public system, even though the cherished autonomy of its institutions makes it sharply different from most of the great state university systems of the West and Middle West. To understand why it looms so large as the shaper of urban and state policy we must first take a look at the enormous range of tasks that The City University must perform. There is a fair accent on the "must" — the university has no option about its involvement with the City of New York. To be a little more precise, City University, unlike its private sisters, has long given up the illusion that it can somehow dream itself out of the great and grim city in which it lives.

City University's first obligation is its oldest, dating back to 1847 when the Free Academy which was to become City College was founded. This is the instruction of undergraduates through to the bachelor's degree. One of the larger ironies (to which New York in its shrug of pride says, "What else is new?") is that the "Harvard of the proletariat" has fulfilled its classic task with so much distinction. There cannot be a faculty of any size in the nation that does not count among its members graduates of City, Hunter, Queens, or Brooklyn colleges; just as, pace Harvard again, there has been no national administration, including the current "middle America" grab bag, which has not poached some of its staff from the same sources. To the four colleges named above can now be added Baruch, Richmond, Lehman, John Jay, and York — all founded (or separated out) within the last decade. City University's dedication to the Whiteheadian task of a university, the confrontation of experience and energy, of learning and imagination, of age and youth goes on. In its size and impersonality, this confrontation mirrors the city itself. And to those who might pine for shaded walks and rural ease, the products of this confrontation answer by matching the city in their toughness, adaptability, and capacity for survival.

A second task is imposed on The City University by the development of American higher education — and that is graduate education. The move of the university into doctoral work created consternation in many circles. Within the university there was the fear that a powerful graduate center would lower the level of instruction in the senior colleges as well as weaken their autonomy. After some eight years of experience, even though these tensions do exist, the fears of the criers of doom have not been justified. Nor is there any longer question that the existence of serious doctoral work within the university can strengthen both faculty recruitment and the integrity of undergraduate offerings. Another cry of doom was raised by the private universities which seem more willing to go broke with graduate programs they cannot afford than to stay in business as undergraduate colleges. The simplest answer to both reactions is usually best; doctoral work will remain as part of The City University of New York because both the city and the university itself need it.

The third responsibility The City University carries is its most clearly practical and least known. New York has a voracious appetite for technicians and professional people — for nurses and teachers, for social workers, policemen, and firemen. The university trains half of the city's teachers, more than half of its nurses, a solid percentage of its social workers, and has an outright monopoly on the collegiate training of both the police and fire departments. In addition, in its seven community colleges, the university provides the city with technically skilled people trained in everything from hotel management to radiation therapy. As new needs develop, the university must help to meet them; for example, its six programs in computer technology. To one appetite it has not yielded; it has no law school.

There are, however, greater needs in a city as complex as New York, needs related not to skills or technologies but to the quality of life itself — some would say to the very possibility of civilized life in the five boroughs. For several generations now the lure of the city has drawn into it a new immigrant wave. But it differs from all the previous waves in that the immigrants are already American citizens when they arrive, although systematically deprived of almost all the skills and attitudes that citizenship should imply. No city can long contain one quarter of its citizens who are deprived not only of its skills and a share of its wealth, but also of hope and of any capacity to care for its welfare. The logical place where citizenship is built is in the schools. But in New York the school system, and thus the city, has failed. Suddenly, then, the city turns to the university and asks it to accept a social challenge greater than and different from any it has faced in the past. Into the desperate cycle of poverty and ignorance that breeds only more poverty and ignorance, and that can only end in destruction, the university is asked to step as poverty interrupter — as the one crack in the wall through which a breakout can be made. The technical name for this interruption is "open admissions," but the reality at stake may well be the viability of the city itself.

One final task remains for this Gargantua of a university. A task it shares with all universities, no matter how large or small. It must live and continue to be; and this means endless questioning of its own forms, structures, and processes. The most immediate questioning of the 1960s was the deep and evident malaise of the students, loudly (and sometimes cryptically) shouting their dissatisfactions with the instructional patterns of the university as well as with the life-styles these patterns impose. In an apparently different direction, the faculty has just moved into the world of labor unions, imposing on itself a startling straitjacket of assumptions, not all of which either the faculty or the university administration has yet caught up with. New procedures and new forms are evidently shaping in the logical vacuum unionization creates, and no one but a fool or a prophet would be willing to guess at their ultimate shapes or results.

As though the two movements listed above were not enough, the university has taken one vast lurch into the social unknown that will inevitably lead it to the deepest questioning of its being it has yet undergone. Instead of its predicted 26,000 freshmen, most of them entering senior colleges with an average of 82 percent or better in their high school work, and all of them holding academic diplomas, the university is prepared to admit next year a total of some 35,000 freshmen. Although the actual plan is somewhat more complicated, it can be summarized by saying that the university will admit, into its senior college system, all applicants who score 80 percent or better, as well as all those who stand in the top half of their high school classes. Its community college system will receive all the rest of the high school graduates, both those scoring under 80 percent and those not in the top half of their individual high school class. Thus, the only requirement for entrance to the university is a high school diploma. In addition, the university is no longer specifying that the diploma must be academic. To meet the new wave of freshmen, and particularly those whose academic preparation is below the standard that the university had previously set, the university must prepare an open-ended freshman year, with a faculty-student ratio of 1 to 10 and a counselor-student ratio of 1 to 50. In addition, it must stretch its already hard-pressed plant with about $5 million worth of rented space, and will have to provide for every student who needs it, specialized help in the form of counseling, remedial work, and tutoring.

This is not the place to detail the number of internal changes and restructurings that this massive freshman class will induce in this and in subsequent years. By opening its doors to the city's minorities The City University has not only accepted a responsibility for remedial education which it could well have spurned as beneath both its capacity and its purpose, but it has also bound itself to a reexamination of that purpose. As a university founded in a world where both cultural and intellectual elitism were taken for granted, City University's open admissions policy drives it counter to exactly those elitist ideas on which it has lived for more than a century. Is it possible to preserve a function with 125 years of tradition and success behind it, and at the same time deny emphatically the "survival-of-the-fittest" social mold in which that function was first created? In more classic terms, can the ambiguous *"agere sequitur esse"* of the scholastics be resolved in favor of an activity which can, in time, determine being? Like Caliban, but with more than one, the university may indeed find its islands "full of noises."

That decision on open admissions begins to show us a major new dimension for the urban public university, and the implications for both American universities and American cities are likely to run far beyond these next few years in New York. By now the history behind the action of the Board of Higher Education (The City University's Board of Trustees) is well known. Open admissions began as a pious wish in the mid-sixties with a safe decade removed between the wish and its fulfillment. As social, economic, and educational forces gathered momentum, the university's schedule was halved and the target date for opening its classrooms to all graduates of the city's high schools was moved up from 1975 to 1970. Every crack in the surface of the city's life showed in the process of that acceleration, but the board's ultimate decision on both timing and method was unanimous.

What is, however, of most interest and of greatest portent was that the decision, made as it was in the middle of a political campaign, was not political. Semantics bedevil one here because it is so deceptively easy to call any decision with political effects, merely political. The causes behind the university's decisions were, however, both deeper and broader. The issues facing the city were too starkly present and too close to its bone for the university to be able to sum them up in terms of either politics or politicians. What prompted the open admissions decision was care for the city itself and for its people. It was a care joined to multiple fears, and to one or two usually unexpressed hopes and dreams. And the world of caring, by any definition, is the world of morality, not of politics. So the university, speaking through its students, its faculty, and ultimately its Board of Trustees, took a position on a major public issue, and took it on the oldest ground known to man, because it was in our time and in our place the right thing to do.

No one involved in the decision, nor in the months of sharp and anguished debate that preceded it, was unaware of the complexities and the risks it involved. Nothing in New York City would ultimately be unaffected by it — for good or for ill. Any success it would have would be haunted by equivocation and the inevitable gap between ideal and reality; and its failure could well be more destructive than anything the city had seen. There were good hopes of success; but there was also the possibility of catastrophe. There were supporters whose motives were patently disruptive, and opponents whose honesty and knowledge could not be questioned. There were fears in the Jewish community that with the new wave of anti-Semitism sweeping through the nation's colleges their last sure educational haven — which they had adopted, dignified, made grow, and flourish — would be denied them; and equal fears in the black community that the entire proposal was just another elaborate hoax and that their children would be left to rot in the ditches the high schools had dug for them. There was no certainty — as there still isn't — that the political forces on which the university must rely for funds would share either its confidence or its order of priorities. Thus like all moral decisions, open admissions was riddled with ambiguities. Despite all this the decision was made.

Of all the agencies through which the official city reaches out toward its people, only the university has dared to take a lead, on moral grounds, and at enormous risk to its ease and comfort. All the other slogans have become jokes. "Safety in the Streets" declines as the police force grows. "Better Hospitals" could be found in medieval France. "Clean Air" is a Republican prerogative to be found from Dutchess County on up. And "Urban Renewal" may work in Manhattan, Kansas, but is likely to leave Manhattan Island evenly divided between stacked offices to the south and slums everywhere else. The university is the major part of the city's apparatus which is, as the students say, vulnerable, and the only one that appears to be capable of response to the city's most cruel human need, the waste of its children.

One conclusion might well be that the major public university, along with being what it always has been, the city's critic and analyst, has now become its social edge as well. If it has, it has also become the one truly mobile part of the vast creaky superstructure that claims to govern and is usually satisfied if the lid stays on. The university will thus have moved, freely and fully, into the arena where things happen, into the kind of social experiment where lives, not ideas are at stake, and where the lives are not only those of the citizens but the life of the city itself. The students may well have been right, as they sometimes are, and for the wrong reason, as we all sometimes are. Gathering her academic robes and her people around her, the old lady of a thousand dreams and ten thousand dreamers has moved off the tenement sill, down the groaning stairs and onto the streets. And having "taken her stand," nothing in or around her will ever be the same.

There can be little question that this deliberate taking of a position is not the modern stance of the American university. When directly attacked, as in the McCarthy days or currently in California, even great universities have known how to gird themselves for a corporate response. But there is little history in this republic of universities taking the initiative — of their deliberately moving out into the public arena. This is even more true when one adds to deliberate motion the assumption of an alien responsibility, the offer to do someone else's job. It is also possible that the whole open admissions decision may be a thing of the moment, parallel to the university response to the Defense Department as the principal source of basic scientific research funds. The carrot was held out, academia ate it, and promptly went back to sleep. So The City University may slide into torpor, although the odds are distinctly against it. And since they are, let us consider the academic results of this university's sudden shift of stance. If having moved out clearly into the public arena she cannot ever move back again, what will change?

One presupposition seems gone forever, and that is the frequently unstated but ever present elitism of the admissions office. The handicappers are not dead by any means, but they have, by the open admissions decision, been given the challenge of their lives. Nor does this challenge stop in the admissions office. It carries through easily into the classroom where the slow paralysis of elitist overspecialization which for three or four generations now has been seeping down from the graduate schools into undergraduate instruction is most clearly to be met. The decision might mean that undergraduate departments will no longer be able to order their teaching and thinking on the premise that all their students are pre-Ph.D.'s; or on the assumption that only pre-Ph.D.'s count and the devil and the draft take the rest. Down from over the department chairman's door can come the sign, "Abandon life all ye who enter here," and English can be taught because literature is fun, history because men are naturally curious, and philosophy because it's a skill necessary for survival. Even the pre-Ph.D.'s won't really be hurt by the experience.

Another casualty of the university's public stance could be the state of chronic intellectual irresponsibility hiding under that slippery Latin word, "objectivity." Any administrator worth his salt knows that the best way to kill a project is to study it, and some of our studies are in fact "quagmires from which no task force has ever returned." Almost any minority community can testify to the modern frustration of being studied always in the interest of a higher wisdom, which cannot be worn or lived in or eaten. "Once the rockets go up who cares where they come down" was more than a satire on one physicist, and with the substitution of "noses" for "rockets" could well be applied to many of our social scientists. It is against this canonization of detachment, reflected not only by individual academics but by whole institutions in their hiring of faculty and others, in their admissions, in their purchasing, in their land policies, in indeed their whole life-styles, that the most strident student protest is aimed. Moving into the public arena means that The City University of New York must shed these hallowed comforts and stand naked to her enemies — at least for a while.

There is one further manifestation of irresponsible objectivism that must also be shed. This is the conscious devaluation of all of Western intellectual currency, "the evacuation of sense and inoperancy of fancy" which has turned our classrooms into ossuary chambers where the nameless bones are fumbled over, caressed, and arranged in brilliantly glistening patterns — all because everyone agrees to forget that they were once meant to hold flesh upright and to bear names and persons through a real world. The de-incarnation of knowledge and of wisdom itself may not be able to survive in a university's inward operations when it no longer suits its corporate and public posture. Perhaps the students were right in first attacking the depersonalized institution as a whole — with the hope that responsibility on the corporate level might help produce some among the individuals in the corporate inclusion, that the breakdown of the university's corporate amoralism might end the private assault on the moral realities of both man and his history. Is it in 1970 too much for those of us who are old enough to know what it means (along with the rebels from the student ranks, who unless we change may never know) to ask that we be made whole again, and that the university help?

That is, however, the interior change that time has already more than half wrought. What concerns us here is the gradual shift in priorities whereby the public university with its thousands of public employees, its millions of public dollars, and its direct impact on the lives of hundreds of thousands of voters, looms as one of the major arms of the establishment, capable in its slow way of moving all the other parts, if it is only willing to move itself. Its principal tool is, of course, negotiation — but it would be a misreading of the times to argue that its present negotiating position is one of weakness. A master of the arts of negotiation once wrote: "If you would work any man, you must either know his nature and fashions, and so lead him; or his ends, and so persuade him; or his weakness and disadvantages, and so awe him; or those that have interest in him, and so govern him."

In dealing with its politicians, the university can safely claim that it understands natures and sets fashions, that it explains ends, that it (lately) serves the disadvantaged, and that it conditions all those likely to care and most of those who will develop interests. Future political scientists may then have a field day criticizing public universities for their success or failure as persuaders and leaders. It can only be hoped that the politicians as well as the academics will have enough sense of humor to spare themselves any professorial efforts to awe or to govern. We may all live to regret the university's sudden emergence into the public world as leader and not follower. The military have long since learned that it is both safer and easier to prepare for the last war. The university may well suffer the same fate and learn to indulge in the same sorry deception. We will be the poorer if it does.

Response to Timothy S. Healy's Paper

By John D. Millett

Ohio has had a statute setting forth in effect an open admissions policy to all state-supported institutions of higher education since 1913. The law reads: "A graduate of the twelfth grade shall be entitled to admission without examination to any college or university which is supported wholly or in part by the state, but for unconditional admission may be required to complete such units in his high school course as may be prescribed, not less than two years prior to his entrance, by the faculty of the institution." The law does go on to say that this section shall not prevent a college of law, college of medicine, or of "other specialized education" to require college training for admission, or prevent a department of art or of music from requiring evidence of "preliminary training or talent."

When I made inquiry into the origins of this legislation, I was told that it was a response to the creation of the College Entrance Examination Board and the beginning of testing as a factor in college admissions. High school principals and superintendents of school districts foresaw that examinations might result in one or both of two consequences: higher education control of the secondary school curriculum and the evaluation of secondary schools in terms of student test performance. In any event, school administrators persuaded the Ohio General Assembly to enact legislation forbidding examination as the basis for admission to state institutions of higher education.[1]

The Ohio law does not explicitly direct state-assisted colleges and universities to admit every high school graduate who presents himself or herself. The law says only that a graduate of the twelfth grade shall be entitled to admission without examination. The statute acknowledges the right of a faculty to fix certain units of high school study as the basis for "unconditional admission." Presumably a student not presenting, let us say, three units of English, two units of science, two units of mathematics, three units of social studies, and two units of a foreign language might be required to take additional courses, not for credit, in order to complete a degree curriculum. The law clearly indicated that it did not apply to graduate school and graduate professional school admission. And at least in the realm of art and music, the law acknowledged that some evidence of talent might be required as a condition of initial admission.

---

1. This account of the origins of the Ohio open admissions law was given to me in the early 1950s by a retired professor of education at Ohio State University. I have never had the opportunity to explore this subject for myself, and I can only repeat the story as told to me.

In practice, however, for nearly 60 years the Ohio law has been generally interpreted as an open admissions law. Public higher education in Ohio has sought to provide an opportunity to every high school graduate who sought entrance into a state-supported college or university. Actually, at least since the end of World War II, there have been various practical constraints that have limited open access in various ways.

Open access is, of course, no promise of academic achievement. As a consequence, the attrition rate among undergraduate students was quite substantial, ranging from 50 to 60 percent of the initial input of freshmen. It was not unusual for Ohio's public institutions to find that the number of students receiving the baccalaureate was around 45 percent of the number of students entering four years before.

In an effort to cut down upon this wastage, various expedients were tried. One was to increase the units of academic study required to be presented by the incoming high school graduate. A second method was to introduce an extensive counseling program. High school graduates who ranked in the lower half of their high school class were invited to come to a campus, to take certain academic aptitude tests, and then to discuss academic objectives with a counselor. No data were ever collected, to my knowledge, about the number of high school graduates thus discouraged from entering a public university, but undoubtedly the number was fairly substantial. If the ill-prepared high school graduate was persistent in his determination to undertake college study, he still had to be admitted, although usually on warning.

Then in the 1950s yet another method of curtailing enrollment demand was discovered. Of the then six state-supported institutions of higher education, only one, the Ohio State University, was located in a major urban area. The other five were located in relatively small communities of from 5,000 to 15,000 population. In these instances the state college or state university had to provide housing for a sizable proportion of its students. In addition, freshmen students other than those living at home with their parents were required to live in university housing where special supervision was expected to help bridge the transition from high school to college study.

University housing was built primarily with borrowed funds, and all operating expenses, including debt service, had to be met from charges to students. The state of Ohio did not provide any capital improvement or current operating appropriations for student housing, or for ancillary social and recreational facilities. It was in the best interest of students, themselves, for a university to assign housing space to students whose academic promise for continued enrollment was relatively high. Otherwise, vacant housing spaces meant higher rents to be charged those students remaining throughout the year. Selective housing assignment thus took the place of selective admission. Indeed, one state university in Ohio became a highly selective institution simply because of this housing circumstance. This selective process did much for the quality of the student body in academic terms.

A major deficiency in Ohio's open admission law was thus demonstrated in these varied experiences. This deficiency simply was the absence of any clear definition of purpose in the open admissions policy. Presumably, the objective of the statute was to serve as an antidote to selective admissions, to provide an opportunity for the high school graduate who might not score high on a test of college aptitude to demonstrate in actual performance his capacity to undertake and complete a baccalaureate curriculum. If academic performance standards set by the faculty were fairly exacting, if program offerings were generally quite academic in content, then the number of students with lower test scores who did in fact demonstrate their capacity for college study remained fairly low.

Under the impetus of statewide higher educational planning, the open admissions policy took on new dimensions in Ohio during the 1960s. The result was an increase of 2½ times in the proportion of young people of college age enrolling in Ohio's public institutions of higher education in 1969 as compared with 1960. The first step was to establish two-year campuses throughout the state, one in every area of 100,000 population and generally within 30 miles of all households. Furthermore, technical education became an important program offering for such two-year campuses, although the expansion of these programs was hampered by some deficiency in facilities and some lack of faculty support. As of 1969 there were about 31 of these two-year campuses. Fees at many of these campuses were around $500 an academic year, and they were accordingly not listed in the recent Carnegie Commission study.

A second step was to create new state-assisted universities in major urban areas of the state. Six new institutions were thus brought into the state system. Three of these had been municipal universities, but limited municipal tax support failed to provide the resources needed for an expansion of student enrollment. Under state financial assistance, increased dollars were available with increased enrollment.

The development of institutions of higher education in urban areas attended primarily upon a commuting basis served to reduce one major obstacle to college enrollment, regardless of the open admissions law. This was the obstacle of financing the costs of housing away from home. These costs were rising steadily during the 1960s under the impact of inflation, the increased expense of borrowing construction funds, and the advancing rates of compensation for food service, housekeeping, and maintenance staffs.

Late in the 1960s, still another factor became apparent in the open admissions law and practice in Ohio. As the interest and concern of black persons to obtain higher education expanded, the open admissions law was an advantage in overcoming any tendency that might have existed to discourage or to discriminate against black students in college enrollment. But as the number of blacks seeking admission increased, it quickly became apparent that open admissions in and of itself had no magic to enable black students to cope with college programs.

New needs quickly became evident. The first was for more extensive student financial assistance. Because many black students came from families of low income and because the opportunities and time available for student employment were limited, black students needed considerable financial support in order to undertake college study. Moreover, in many instances black students found it advantageous to enroll on a residential basis in order to get away from disadvantageous home conditions. But this meant that housing as well as all other expenses of college attendance had to be provided. With federal programs of student financial assistance undergoing some contraction under the impact of the Vietnam war, there was no alternative except for the state to begin to provide student financial assistance.

Financial assistance was only a part of the need, however. There were deficiencies in secondary school preparation also to be overcome. Various efforts were necessary. Remedial courses in English and in mathematics were offered in the summer quarter to high school students as a means of improving learning capabilities. School principals and superintendents acknowledged the need for this assistance and generally tended to support it. After the student actually entered college, other reinforcing efforts were needed: counseling about learning skills, special tutoring, special courses, and new programs of instruction "relevant" to the black experience and aspiration.

I do not wish to be understood as suggesting that any of our efforts in Ohio have been adequate to the needs of black students or that they have accomplished great miracles in enabling black students to perform on a satisfactory accomplishment level in competition with other students. We have had sufficient experience to date, I believe, to say that massive efforts are required if open admissions is to be helpful to a good many black students. Furthermore, we are beginning to accumulate some evidence, I believe, that such massive efforts can be of assistance to certain black students in overcoming educational disadvantages experienced prior to college enrollment. Motivation continues to be a major factor in academic performance.

It must be emphasized again that open admissions as a state law and as a state policy is only a means to an end. It can serve as a means of overcoming any injustices arising from a selective admissions practice. It can serve as a means of overcoming racial obstacles to college enrollment. Yet in and of itself, open admissions is only a start in overcoming barriers to higher education: barriers of geographical location of institutions of higher education, barriers of financial expense in attending colleges and universities, barriers in preparation for college study, barriers in program operation.

The critical issue in open admissions remains that of standards of performance expected in a college or university. Presumably some standards of performance will continue to be maintained, and these standards will be such that not every young person will be able to meet them. Open admissions does not necessarily mean the abandonment of standards of academic performance in our institutions of higher education. Open admissions does mean a continuing appraisal of these standards in relation to the various intellectual, manpower, and social objectives of higher education.

Predicting College Success of Educationally Disadvantaged Students[1]

By Julian C. Stanley

Because children of the poor tend to score lower on the Scholastic Aptitude Test and other standardized ability and achievement tests than do children of the affluent, one can say that *in this descriptive sense* such tests are "biased against" or "discriminate against" or "penalize" the former. Besides their descriptive denotations, however, these expressions have value connotations. Are such tests "unfair" to youth from educationally disadvantaging environments? The answer depends, of course, on what is meant in this context by the word "unfair."

During the first half of the past decade a number of writers questioned the validity of standardized tests for ascertaining the abilities of lower-socio-economic-group children. One of these was President Martin Jenkins (1964) of predominantly black Morgan State College in Baltimore, who wrote: ". . . it is well known that standardized examinations have low validity for individuals and groups of restricted experiential background." That same year Joshua Fishman and others (1964, p. 130), presenting the "Guidelines for Testing Minority Group Children" of the Society for the Psychological Study of Social Issues (SPSSI), wrote that the "predictive validity [of standardized tests currently in use] for minority groups may be quite different from that for the standardization and validation groups . . ."

A year earlier Clark and Plotkin (1963) had reported results of a study based on "alumni" classes of the National Scholarship Service and Fund for Negro Students in which they concluded that ". . . scholastic aptitude test scores are

---

1. An earlier version of this paper appeared as *Report No. 79* of the Center of Social Organization of Schools, The Johns Hopkins University, September 1970.

not clearly associated with college grades. It is suggested that college admissions officers weigh test scores less, since they do not predict the college success of Negro students in the same way they do for whites. This study indicates that motivational factors are probably more important than test scores in the demonstrated superiority of Negro students in completing college.''

In 1965 Green and Farquhar reported an r of only .01 between School and College Ability Test scores (level not specified) and high school grade-point averages for 104 black males, compared with .62 for the Differential Aptitude Test verbal-reasoning scores of 254 white males.

Do these excerpts prove that standardized tests indeed have lower predictive validity for educationally disadvantaged college students than for others? By no means, as extensive reviews by Stanley and Porter (1967), Thomas and Stanley (1969), Kendrick and Thomas (1970), Ruch (1970), and Jensen (1970), and articles by Boney (1966), Cleary (1968), Hills and Stanley (1968 and in press), Wilson (1969), and others show. Only the Clark and Plotkin and Green and Farquhar studies, of those excerpted above, dealt with data. Cleary tried to replicate the findings of Clark and Plotkin with a better controlled design, but failed. The conclusions of Green and Farquhar are questioned in some detail by Stanley and Porter. For black students, especially, the differential-validity hypothesis has been found untenable, except that sometimes test scores *over*predict the academic achievement of the disadvantaged.

For further background see Mitchell (1967), Lennon (1968), Educational Testing Service (1969), and APA Task Force on Employment Testing of Minority Groups (1969).

An Analogous Situation

Let us try to examine the implied logic that leads to assertions such as those made by Jenkins (1964), Fishman et al. (1964), and Clark and Plotkin (1963). We can start with an extreme analogy, using measured height as the "test score" and ability to sink baskets in basketball as the criterion.

Suppose that a short ninth-grader approaches the basketball coach and says something such as the following: "I know that I'm not as tall as any player on the high school team, but you must make special allowances for me because I never had the opportunity to reach my full height potential. My parents were so poor that even during my mother's pregnancy she did not have an adequate diet. Had I been fed as well as those middle-class boys on the team I'd be as tall as the typical one of them."

The coach might reply: "Yes, maybe you would have been, but in fact you aren't tall enough to play basketball on this team unless either you can sink baskets as well as the taller boys can or we can find some way such as an enriched diet to increase your height. I doubt that you can compete with those fellows at your present height. Nevertheless I will give you a brief chance to demonstrate whether or not you can. Also, I have little confidence that at your age we can increase your height greatly, relative to other boys, but of course we can try that, too.''

Height in the example is a measure of development at a certain age. From it one cannot infer potential directly. The height score does not tell us *why* the boy is short. Also, the known height, even in conjunction with the boy's assertions about prolonged, severe malnutrition, does not tell us what the prognosis for increased height is. That is an empirical issue which depends on the methods attempted and the laws of physiology. Within the boy there is no height homunculus waiting to leap upward. There is no pristine ''height potential'' that has lingered from the point of conception, always waiting to be actualized. One might have to work very hard to increase the boy's height-rank among his peers even a little. It might be more efficient to improve his basket-sinking skill (that is, make him an ''overachiever''), but without the necessary height he may not even then become adept enough to play well on that team. Perhaps he can join a team of shorter players, where his height falls within the range of his teammates.

Admittedly, some intellectual abilities may not be nearly as difficult to improve at age 14 or 18 as height probably is, but the underlying principles seem the same. Suppose that one has two large groups of high school seniors, and that the score on the verbal sections of the Scholastic Aptitude Test (SAT) of every person in each group is, say, 400. Suppose, further, that one group is composed of students from inner-city slums; their parents are poorly educated, and most middle-class educational influences are missing from their homes. The students who make up the other group are from affluent suburbs, and most of their parents are college graduates. (To keep the argument uncluttered, let us assume that each student's 400 is essentially his true score, the average of half a dozen SAT verbal scores. Then regression toward population means because of errors of measurement will not complicate this discussion. Also, assume that both groups had plenty of experience with tests prior to taking the SAT.)

Which group's scores should be easier to increase? Intuitively, one responds immediately, ''The slum group's, because those students had little educational stimulation at home or in the community. Stimulation should work wonders.'' As with height, however, this is an empirical issue. Even assuming that at the time of conception the disadvantaged youth had greater potential than the nondisadvantaged youth for scoring high on the verbal sections of the SAT, it does not follow that this potential persists undiminished to age 17 or 18. Perhaps the disadvantaged seniors are so stunted intellectually that massive coaching, tutoring, remediation, and enrichment won't raise most of their SAT-verbal scores much. Perhaps such efforts will raise them appreciably, but one has to specify the methods to be used and actually try them out.

Coaching to Improve Test Scores

Not enough of this has been done yet in a rigorous way and reported, but the study by Roberts and Oppenheim (1966) should alert optimists to be more cautious in their expectations. After conducting an experiment using the Preliminary Scholastic Aptitude Test with 720 eleventh-grade students in 18 predominantly black schools, they concluded that: "The outcome of this study, like those of earlier studies [see College Entrance Examination Board, 1968b] investigating whether coaching can raise aptitude test scores, is essentially negative. The performance of the experimental groups proved to be lower than was expected. Nevertheless, the question of whether one can intervene effectively to supplement the *instruction* of the culturally deprived high school student persists. Future investigations might concentrate upon the particular learning problems of this population and what techniques might prove to be effective to overcome these problems rather than take the form of additional coaching studies as they have been performed in the past." [Italics added.]

Alternative Coping Skills

Even when it is recognized that educators do not know how to increase the tested SAT-verbal ability of disadvantaged high school juniors or seniors appreciably, it is often contended those students do not need as much of this ability as more advantaged students do in order to succeed in college. Seldom is it asked why they would not need more ability. The contender seems to imply that students who have come up the rough way will study harder and more effectively than advantaged students, or perhaps even that by having survived in the ghetto they have developed coping techniques useful also in schools. Of course, these speculations do not square well with the many other disadvantages besides test-score deficits that the slum-bred students have, nor with the facts of their usual academic difficulties in elementary and high school. If strong motivation to achieve academically is there, it must in most instances be lying dormant, ready to spring forth in college. One might expect, or at least hope for, satisfactory college work from a person who has earned good grades in high school college-preparatory courses *or* has high-enough test scores. However, to expect good college grades from most students who have neither is asking for a minor academic miracle, unless sufficiently massive compensatory education intervenes. Such miracles do happen from time to time, but there does not seem to be any credible evidence that they occur frequently or when the gaps to be leaped are great.

Persistence to Graduation

A tactic recently adopted at a number of academically selective colleges is to emphasize the disadvantaged student's persistence, rather than his grades. For example, at Cornell University Tetlow (1969) found that the 56 students who scored below the fifth percentile "of all entering Cornell students for the undergraduate division in question" on 2 out of 3 of SAT-verbal, SAT-mathematical, and secondary school class rank "are doing extremely well with regards to academic status, and if the trend continues, about 90 percent will graduate and less than 5 percent will be academically dismissed." (At Cornell the fifth percentile on SAT-verbal scores in the College of Arts and Sciences is about 535, so most of the students who score in the lowest 5 percent there are far above the national median SAT-verbal score of high school graduates.)

In another part of the report, Dr. Tetlow shows that the average grades of the entire group of presumably high-risk students at Cornell were rather low and that "about half of all students in the program have received *at least* a warning for poor performance. Several students have received a 'warning,' a 'final warning,' and a 'post-final warning.'" Clearly, more than just persistence to graduation must be demonstrated if such a program is to be considered a success. What have these students *learned* by the time they graduate, for example, as measured by the aptitude, achievement, and area tests of the Graduate Record Examination? Would they have learned more had they attended a less academically demanding college where with the same amount of effort they could have made better grades?

In an important study Astin (1970) has used a persistence argument, too, though his pooling of grades across 180 colleges of various selectivity levels makes some of his conclusions difficult to interpret. He matched ingeniously, also, but within-college analyses would have been more convincing. His findings may have little necessary relevance to disadvantaged students *recruited* into selective colleges, but they do suggest considerable persistence in college by many students with weak academic backgrounds.

A large study of persistence to graduation at Brown University was reported by Nicholson (1970). His data and conclusions are interesting, although his definition of a high-risk student (that is, one whose SAT-verbal score is less than 620) screens in few really educationally disadvantaged persons.

Studies of persistence were also conducted by Clark and Plotkin (1963) and Borgen (1970).

Not many systematic studies of differential persistence of blacks versus whites have yet been completed, but the evidence from Clark and Plotkin, Tetlow, Astin, Borgen, and Nicholson suggests that reasonably able black students from high socioeconomic backgrounds who attend selective colleges persist well to graduation, even though many of them make mediocre or poor grades. Most of these students were self-selected into the colleges, however, rather than being recruited strongly. Also, they had rather few black classmates with whom to isolate themselves from the whites or with whom to agitate for black courses, curriculums, departments, and colleges. This situation has changed rapidly within the last few years, so the older data can be suggestive only, and just for blacks. We know virtually nothing yet concerning the persistence of other disadvantaged minority groups.

The relationship of parental socioeconomic level to academic persistence transcends the race issue. For example, at the University of Illinois, Eckland (1964a, 1964b) found that for persistence to obtaining a degree somewhere within a 10-year period following initial enrollment "social class is an important determinant . . . for students from the lower rank of their high school classes but relatively unimportant for those from the higher rank . . ." Giving up pursuit of the degree did not seem closely related to lack of money; those who dropped out for what they said were financial reasons tended to return and graduate. Lack of money is a real handicap, but at least in principle a remediable one.

Mere persistence to the award of a degree cannot, of course, be the primary criterion. The persister must in the process be getting at least as good an education as he could secure elsewhere for the same effort and cost. Careful evaluation of the attainments of the students as they progress seems imperative.

Ignoring Test Scores

Recently, many selective institutions have decided to waive test scores (and sometimes high school grades, too) in admitting disadvantaged applicants. If the rationale for this is that the College Board Scholastic Aptitude Test and Achievement Tests lower prediction of criteria such as freshman grade-point average or persistence to graduation, it is a foolish procedure, because in a multiple-regression equation a predictor variable cannot lower validity, but only increase it or leave it unchanged. (Nonlinear regression might work differently, but it is quite unlikely to occur when the usual academic predictors are employed, as Lee showed in 1957.) Substituting principals' and teachers' ratings of probable college success for test scores and high school grades appears to be a step backward into the pre-1906 era of college selection. Rather, it would seem more sensible to predict the criterion (usually grade-point average or persistence) for each applicant using all available predictors, and then, if desired, to set up predictive lists separately for disadvantaged and nondisadvantaged applicants. Those disadvantaged applicants who on the basis of all evidence seem most promising, academically and otherwise, can be invited to attend college, offered financial aid and, where needed, provided massive educational facilitation.

I would urge a reversal of the current trend. *The more disadvantaged an applicant seems to be socioeconomically, the greater amount of objective information one needs about him.* What are his weaknesses and his strengths? How, for instance, does he score on several College Board Achievement Tests? Does he have some special developed academic ability or other relevant aptitude? It is well to consider noncognitive measures, too, but not in lieu of the cognitive ones.

Especially disturbing is the tendency to ignore test scores and put the main reliance on the high school academic record. As Thomas and Stanley (1969) have reported, and as Thomas is now studying further as the basis for his doctoral dissertation at The Johns Hopkins University, ''. . . high school grades do not consistently make the greatest contribution in predicting college grades of black students, perhaps particularly of men, whereas they do for whites. Unreliability of grade reporting, invalidity of grades in high school, restriction in range due to selection processes, and intergroup differences in personality characteristics [are] advanced to explain this phenomenon.''

Predictive Validity

As noted earlier, aptitude test scores and high school grades, when used together, usually do predict college grades of disadvantaged applicants about as well as they do for regular ones. This is a carefully verified general finding, but of course it depends on the relative range of talent in the two groups. At Cornell, for instance, first-semester r's for the special-program students tended to be lower than for all arts and sciences freshmen; however, data for the former were from a pooled four-year period, whereas for the latter they were for a single year. Heterogeneity of grades and grading across the years may have lowered the r's (see Tetlow, 1969, Table 5). Also, although there is no way to tell from the report how comparatively homogeneous the two groups are, it seems quite likely that test scores and perhaps high school grades of the special-program students were considerably less variable than were those of the regularly admitted students. If so, much of the difference in r's was probably due to restriction of range, rather than to invalidity of the tests. A single regression equation might predict college grades equally well for the two races there.

Many claims that test scores have little or no value for predicting the ''success'' of disadvantaged applicants to colleges are made. Anecdotes are abundant (for example, see Somerville, 1967), but usually upon investigation they cannot be verified or they prove to be atypical. *An admissions officer ignores test scores at his institution's peril.* Test scores certainly are useful most of the time for helping to predict college grades, and also are probably useful for helping predict which students who persist through a highly permissive selective college will come out with an education, rather than just a quickly discredited union card.

Biased Items?

The larger issue of item "bias" was attacked vigorously but rather unsuccessfully in the early 1950s by Eells and others (1951). Those investigators worked hard to devise a "culture-fair" test, one that would still be predictively valid but that would not discriminate so sharply between socioeconomic classes as, for example, the Otis Test of Mental Ability does. Its situations and items, incorporated into the Davis-Eells "Games," were slanted toward urban slum cultures; nevertheless, the new test served as about as effective a differentiator of socioeconomic classes as its culturally "unfair" predecessors had. (For example, see Ludlow, 1956.)

A more recent study by Cleary and Hilton (1968) revealed a statistically significant but small interaction of race (black versus white) with the items of two forms of the Preliminary Scholastic Aptitude Test (PSAT). As Stanley (1969c) showed later, a considerable amount of this interaction was due to a few items that were too difficult for both races and hence did not separate them much. There seemed little likelihood that one could find in either subtest (verbal or mathematical) of the PSAT a subset of item types especially favorable or unfavorable to the blacks, who scored rather uniformly lower than the whites on most of the items.

For a long time it has been well known to specialists that blacks score relatively higher on verbal items than they score on nonverbal ones (for example, see Lesser, Fifer, and Clark, 1965, and Stodolsky and Lesser, 1967). Hence, attempts to create valid culture-fair tests by reducing their verbal content have slight chance of being successful. One can, of course, find tests such as speed of tapping that may not differentiate socioeconomic levels or races well, but such tests probably will not predict desired academic criteria adequately, either.

Where the criteria are loaded in certain ways—"biased," if you insist—the predictors must be loaded similarly if they are to correlate well with those criteria. If the criteria change (for example, from grades to persistence with any minimal academic record whatsoever), the predictors must be changed accordingly.

Tacitly Different Criteria

It follows almost as a corollary that if the correlation of certain fixed predictors with a criterion is different for one group versus another, the *criterion itself* may well be different for the two groups, even though it has the same name (for example, grade-point ratio or receiving a diploma). For example, to predict persistence to graduation of "high-risk" applicants to a college may require considerable knowledge of the grading practices, liberal tendencies, "gut" courses, and fail-safe curriculums within the institution. Also, one may need quite different, or at least differently weighted, predictors of persistence to graduation of disadvantaged applicants than for predicting Achievement-Test scores of those students in May of their senior year.

Following Up Dropouts and Persisters

In an important sense, the percentage of a college's entering freshmen who persist to graduation there in four or five years may be an excellent measure of its selective and nurturing efficiency. This should, it seems to me, be supplemented by careful assessment of what each graduate has learned and what each does subsequently. High-risk entrants can be treated separately from regular ones. Dropouts can be followed so that the quitters can be separated from the transferers. With excellent computer facilities in many institutions and the work of Eckland (1964a, 1964b) as an early example, perhaps many colleges will broaden their criteria beyond first-semester or first-year grade-point average. Getting through to a degree is a kind of sine qua non, but obtaining at least as good an education as one might have secured with the same expenditure of money and energy elsewhere is crucial. I fear that in the rather frantic recruitment of disadvantaged students, especially blacks, into selective colleges and universities their education itself may sometimes have been lost sight of.

Academic Frustration

If the SAT, additional College Board tests, and other such instruments measure essentially the same developed abilities for the disadvantaged and advantaged, as they indeed seem to do, and if at least a certain minimum level of such abilities is virtually essential for success in a given college, how can students far below the barely acceptable level of a given college avoid being seriously frustrated academically there? This is not a question of color or ethnic background, but instead a question of academic competence, and of course the student's prior grades in school must usually be weighted heavily in assessing that competence.

If your son or mine scores 400 on both the verbal and mathematical sections of the SAT, and ranks far below the top of his high school class, he is a poor academic bet for highly selective colleges such as Cal Tech, Harvard, Stanford, and Swarthmore. Wise parents would not want him to go there, even if by some leniency or error he were to be admitted. It is not that he could not *possibly* pass carefully selected courses there and get some sort of degree; a *few* heroically motivated persons at that level might. Rather, we would fear that trying to compete far above his comfortable level would confine him to the easier courses and curriculums, thereby limiting his choice. Also, though he might scrape through most of his courses with Cs and Ds, what would he be learning, compared to what he might learn in another college where his relative level of ability is average or better? And what sort of academic self-concept would he be developing? With these considerations in mind, probably we would urge him to attend a college more geared to his level of academic competence. Not many colleges in the United States are highly selective. There exist at least 2,000 others of all sorts to accommodate most levels of developed ability and achievement.

Enrollees Quite Underqualified Academically

A considerable number of minority-group students with weak academic preparation are being recruited vigorously into the most selective colleges and universities in the country; there the test scores of many such recruits may be several standard deviations below the average nonspecial student, and even far below the *minimum* level for regular admission to the institution. Also, their high school education and achievement are typically an additional handicap. Most colleges do not publish comparative figures for special students versus regularly admitted students, but by being diligent one can get a few statistics such as the following:

Kendrick (1968, p. 8) infers from the Coleman Report that *"not more than 15 percent and perhaps as few as 10 percent of . . . Negro high school seniors would score 400 or more on the verbal section of the* SAT. *Only 1 or 2 percent would be likely to score 500 or more"* (italics his). For all high school seniors in the country the percentages are approximately 45 and 20, respectively (College Entrance Examination Board, 1968a, p. 23). Thus the number of black high school graduates each year who have well-developed verbal ability is quite small. As noted earlier (Tetlow, 1969), the fifth percentile of SAT-verbal scores for freshmen in the College of Arts and Sciences at Cornell University is 535. Brown University (Nicholson, 1970, p. 3) uses a cutoff of 620 on the SAT-verbal scores to define those students who are considered academic risks there! "Such a point defines approximately the lower one-third of currently admitted students . . ."

Cornell University may have the ablest large group of black college students in the country, if scores on the Scholastic Aptitude Test are used as the criterion. In an undated booklet entitled *Expanding Opportunities for Minority Groups* (Cornell University, circa 1968, p. 6) the verbal means of the special-program (chiefly black) entering freshmen for 1965–66 through 1968–69 are shown to range from 530 to 570, whereas the College of Arts and Sciences freshmen range from 660 to 703; the average difference between the blacks and the entire arts and sciences group was 137 points. No standard deviations are given, but this difference seems likely to be nearly two standard deviations of the black group. The lowest SAT-verbal scores for the 247 blacks were reported by year as 430, 340, 400, and 383.

In the fall of 1967 Michigan State University enrolled "66 not-normally admissible Negro freshmen . . . [m]ore than half [of whom] had combined Scholastic Aptitude Test scores [that is, verbal plus mathematical] of under 789" (Sabine, 1968, pp. 11, 14). No comparative figures for regularly admitted freshmen are given, but the following informal remarks by Dr. Sabine on page 13 indicate the discrepancy: "May 28 [1968]: Lunch with four faculty members who want to 'do something,' meaning tutor Negro freshmen next fall. Their ideas are good, and all went well until they started saying how high the student's grades and test scores should be. They had a hard time believing we haven't even one that high in our special-admission group."

For the University of Illinois during the academic year 1968–69 Humphreys (1969) reported "a difference between the means of the two races that was 2.4 times the standard deviation of the Caucasian distribution." Bowers (1970) provides detailed comparisons of the 111 men and 152 women in the Special Educational Opportunities Program (SEOP) with the regular Illinois freshmen on eight test variables and high school rank. For the latter, the SEOP students were considerably below the regular students, also. Admissions officers have known for many years that a double handicap of this kind (that is, ranking low on *both* aptitude and high school record within an entering class) makes for a pessimistic academic prognosis.

Humphreys (1969) forcefully stated the dilemma Illinois faced: "There will be an intolerable level of dropping of Negro students on academic grounds during the first year unless there is *massive* intervention. A desirable form of intervention is to establish special sections and special remedial courses. An undesirable form is for the faculty to assign grades in regular racially mixed classes on the basis of skin color rather than performance. In the present emotional climate, if more desirable forms of intervention are not *sufficiently massive,* this second type becomes inevitable.

"There is another effect of bringing in Negro students who are *far* below their fellow students in readiness to do academic work. A group of young people who are newly imbued with pride in race are placed in a situation in which they are, by and large, obviously inferior. A scientist qualifies this inferiority by adding 'at their present stage of development,' but this is slight consolation to the student involved. The causal chain from frustration to aggression is well established. *A large ability difference as a source of aggression cannot be ignored.* The universities are damned if they don't admit more Negroes, but they are also damned in another sense if they do." [Italics added.]

Academic Frustration Accentuates Demands for Relevance?

Stanley (1969a, 1969b, 1970) is more pessimistic than Humphreys about the efficacy of remediation, tutoring, and coaching during the freshman year for overcoming *large* gaps. Also, he suspects that demands for "relevant" "black" courses and instructors are to a considerable extent probably unconscious rationalizations of pressures of competition with regular students who are much better qualified academically. If the available curriculums are too difficult, students must demand easier curriculums, fail, or leave. One's pride is saved, however, by not admitting (even to oneself) how almost impossibly difficult the regular courses and curriculums are, but instead pride is saved by searching for nobler-sounding motives. Some statements by a black assistant dean of students at Cornell University and her assistant (Joseph and Newsom, 1968) are relevant to this conjecture: "[The black students'] interest in making sure that their course work is relevant — a word they use with even more frequency than white students — has *the fervor of a religious cause.* It is not, however, a "white" relevance they seek . . . [A black student] commented, "Most courses aren't interesting to me. I find it difficult to study them. They are relevant to white students, but not to black students." . . . They define relevant courses as those taught by Negroes . . . or by professors who understand and take account of the Negro contribution and point of view . . . [B]y far the largest number are in the College of Arts and Sciences. And there it is courses in economics, sociology, psychology, and the humanities that *arouse their passions* most." [Italics added.]

Are "white physics," "white engineering," and "white premed" deemed irrelevant largely because they are too difficult for many specially admitted students? It is not easy to assess the contribution of academic unreadiness to demands for segregated curriculums, departments, and colleges; however, recent events at a number of colleges seem consonant with the interpretation that it plays more than a minor role in activities which effectively reduce the competition with better-prepared students.

Less-Selective Colleges Need Assistance

A dilemma is that power, resources, and good will seem to reside chiefly at the academically difficult institutions, whereas the real higher education opportunities for many of the disadvantaged are at state colleges, certain private colleges, community colleges, and the less selective state universities. Over the years of this century the principle that a high school graduate will usually be wise to attend a college neither extremely difficult nor extremely easy for him seems to have been validated rather thoroughly. The educationally disadvantaged should be treated as individuals, and not as a species apart from the advantaged. They — especially blacks, Mexican Americans, American Indians, and Puerto Ricans on the mainland — deserve special consideration and special treatment: financial aid, remediation and tutoring, reduced course loads, extended probation, counseling, and so on. There is, however, no magic in a degree from a usually selective college if it is not in one's preferred field, if it represents little real educational attainment, or if the recipient has convinced himself that he is stupid and convinced others that his entire racial or ethnic group is vastly inferior to the typical students in the college.

We need massive federal and local aid to put resources such as scholarships, loans, and counselors where they are most likely to yield the greatest educational increments. A number of persons, among them economist John D. Owen (1970), are devising model federal scholarship programs that will include the disadvantaged. It should be unnecessary for those disadvantaged students who prefer not to major in racial or ethnic politics or social studies to attend a prestigious, highly selective college in order to get financial support because a more appropriately difficult college can help them little financially.

Admission and Facilitation

Nothing in this paper should be taken to mean that I believe that no students from disadvantaging backgrounds should be in selective colleges. Clearly, some of them will be well served academically, socially, and emotionally there. *I advocate treating each college applicant as an individual, rather than primarily as a member of a group.* Logically, that leads to essentially "color-blind" and "ethnic-blind" *admission* to college, though minority-group members at the low end of the normally admissible applicant group can be given special consideration for admission and much facilitation if enrolled. Admissions of applicants quite academically underqualified for the particular college as it presently exists will necessitate new, easier *curriculums* for that college — not just "massive" remediation and tutoring.

High school rank in class, academic-aptitude test scores, and achievement test scores are still the best predictors of grades the applicant would earn in a particular college and, probably, of his fruitful persistence there. I do not know any convincing evidence that different predictors or even differently weighted predictors of current criteria of academic success are needed for the disadvantaged versus the advantaged. Probably more test information is needed about the disadvantaged than about the advantaged, as discussed earlier.

For the public schools, McPartland (1970) has concluded that the presence of a high percentage of academic and value pacesetters within the individual classroom is essential for stimulating the disadvantaged to greater achievement. If his findings are applicable to colleges, many pacesetters in the classes seem needed, but the disadvantaged students should not be almost hopelessly outclassed.

McPartland does not think that a mixture of whites with blacks is in principle educationally crucial, however, because he wrote: "There is no question but that the desegregated Negro students could have experienced the same kinds of rewards and gains had they switched from the usual segregated school to another all-black school which enrolled students from highly educated and economically advantaged families. In practical terms, though, there simply are not presently enough advantaged black families to accomplish social-class desegregation without racial desegregation" (p. 22).

Predicting Occupational Level

It is easy to be persuaded that school grades and test scores do not predict "life success." There is a basic flaw in such an argument, as a few examples will illustrate. Suppose you know the Stanford-Binet IQs of a group of children, as Lewis Terman did in his famed "genius" study. If their IQs range from 140 upward, averaging 150, would you predict their adult occupational level to be average? Of course not. (See Terman and Oden, 1947.) Analogously, what is the probability that out of 1,000 carefully tested eight-year-old boys who have IQs of 90 there will emerge even one Ph.D.-level mathematician, or Shakespearian scholar?

Suppose that for the year 1950 high school graduating classes of 100 students or more, you knew the names and present addresses of three males in each class, the top-ranking one, the one who ranked nearest the middle, and the one who ranked nearest the bottom. Subsequent education, occupational level, and even income would quite likely be found to differ considerably among the three groups in the predicted direction.

The usual fallacy in this type of argument arises because it seems to be true that among those persons who, for instance, exactly complete high school — *no more and no less* — it is difficult to find strong correlations of grades or test scores with measures of life success. Reflect, though, that by eliminating those who drop out before high school graduation and those who attend college, the group has been homogenized considerably with respect to motivation, socioeconomic status, intellectual ability, and many other characteristics. That restricts predictive possibilities greatly. Grades and test scores are rather potent predictors of continuation in school, which in turn leads to increased occupational level and, usually, also to increased lifetime earnings (but not invariably, of course, because for example a plumber may have a larger annual income than a physicist, and begin drawing it four or more years earlier).

Increasing Educational Mobility

It may pay us to view the central problem more broadly. How can intergenerational educational mobility be fostered? How can the children of the uneducated poor of any race or ethnic background be given a better educational chance than they will usually get if not aided? Many such children suffer compound disadvantagement: educationally unstimulating homes, poorly developing academic abilities, lack of financial resources, and community influences (especially including peers) that are educationally disabling. Our nation is struggling with the problems of helping such youngsters develop their abilities and school motivation better from the point of conception onward. Much more must be done far earlier than the eleventh or twelfth grade if efforts there are to become increasingly successful. A current dilemma is that our present knowledge and funds all along the line are so limited that we tend to cream off the top of the nominally disadvantaged groups. We do not often get down to the really disadvantaged. They present so many problems of finance, motivation, and curriculum that we tend to fight over the more malleable slightly disadvantaged instead.

That word "disadvantaged" gets us into trouble, anyway. From the standpoint of the admissions officer of a given college, who are the educationally disadvantaged? Perhaps they are simply those applicants to his college who, on the basis of all available information including socioeconomic status, race, ethnic origin, and available financial support, are likely to have appreciably more academic difficulty than the typical minimally admissible student. From this viewpoint, the son of a distinguished alumnus is "disadvantaged" if he is predicted to fail most of his courses and not persist to graduation. The brilliant high school valedictorian whose parents are illiterate and penniless but who has a sizable national scholarship cannot, by this criterion, be considered disadvantaged. Likewise, the high-achieving son of a black physician cannot be considered educationally disadvantaged simply because of his color.

Definition of collegiate disadvantagement as a low predicted grade-point average, based on all available antecedent information, immediately alerts the institution to compensatory action that must be taken quickly if the applicant is admitted. How much financial aid will it take to improve the academic prognosis sufficiently? If the applicant is black and from an educationally and socially disadvantaging background compared to the usual freshmen at the college, what must be done to improve his academic chances there? If he is from a remote part of Appalachia, what facilitation does he need?

This rationale makes the expression "educationally disadvantaged" or "high risk" more than a euphemism for "minority-group member." It goes beyond the peeling paint on the house or the father's poor education to assess more directly the educational promise of the applicant with all his handicaps and assets, and his probable achievement if some of the handicaps can be removed.

Conclusion

In this paper I have covered, usually too briefly, many more topics than the title promised. It is a complex area, and current practice often seems to me unwise. This decade will tell about that, however. The many open-admissions programs can be informative, though perhaps often traumatically or even chaotically so. Because of delicate political considerations, objective evidence from most of them will be ruled out for all except a few concerned insiders. If the College Board can devise ways to collect and share information from the many special programs without jeopardizing the positions of perhaps insecurely placed persons who administer them, it may hasten needed corrective measures. Meanwhile, we must rely mainly on news media, within-college reports, public relations releases, and an occasional article in a journal such as the *College Board Review,* or a paper at a professional meeting to discern vaguely how effective educationally the special programs actually are.

Summary

Test scores predict the college grades of blacks at least as well as they do those of whites. High school grades considerably augment the prediction for both groups. Students, regardless of socioeconomic level, who are predicted to earn quite low grades within a particular college will tend to have academic difficulties if enrolled in it. There is social and educational justification for admitting to a particular college some minority-group students who are marginally qualified for it academically, *provided that* they are given adequate financial aid and effective remedial courses, tutoring, and coaching. If entrants are *greatly* underqualified academically for a particular college, however, new curriculums will be required. These may tend to segregate the specially admitted students from the regular student body and thereby diminish the pacesetter role of the latter. Also, a degree from a special curriculum may not be viewed by employers, graduate schools, and alumni as equivalent to the other degrees awarded by the institution. Thus, admitting students who are seriously underqualified academically for a particular college seems likely to cause frustrations that may be difficult to resolve. Current demands by minority groups for "relevant" courses may reflect the academic difficulties many of their members encounter in present courses more than the long-term educational unsuitability for them of such courses.

References

APA Task Force on Employment Testing of Minority Groups, "Job Testing and the Disadvantaged." *American Psychologist,* Vol. 24, 1969, pp. 637–650.

Astin, Alexander W., "Racial Considerations in Admissions," in David C. Nichols and Olive Mills (eds.), *The Campus and the Racial Crisis.* Washington, D.C.: American Council on Education, 1970, pp. 113–141.

Boney, J. Don, "Predicting the Academic Achievement of Secondary School Negro Students." *Personnel and Guidance Journal,* Vol. 44, 1966, pp. 700–703.

Borgen, Fred. H., "Able Black Americans in College: Entry and Freshman Experiences." *National Merit Scholarship Corporation Research Reports,* Vol. 6, No. 2, 1970.

Bowers, John (University of Illinois), *Factor Structures and Predictive Validities of College Ability Tests for Regularly Admitted and Disadvantaged Beginning Freshmen at the University of Illinois.* Paper read at the American Educational Research Association convention, Minneapolis, Minnesota, March 3, 1970.

Clark, Kenneth B., and Plotkin, Lawrence, *The Negro Student at Integrated Colleges.* New York: National Scholarship Service and Fund for Negro Students, 1963, p. 9.

Cleary, T. Anne, "Test Bias: Prediction of Grades of Negro and White Students in Integrated Colleges." *Journal of Educational Measurement,* Vol. 5, No. 2, 1968, pp. 115–124.

Cleary, T. Anne, and Hilton, Thomas L., "An Investigation of Item Bias." *Educational and Psychological Measurement,* Vol. 28, 1968, pp. 61–75.

College Entrance Examination Board, *College Board Score Reports, 1968–69.* New York: College Entrance Examination Board, 1968a.

College Entrance Examination Board, *Effects of Coaching on Scholastic Aptitude Test Scores.* New York: College Entrance Examination Board, 1968b.

Cornell University, *Expanding Opportunities for Minority Groups: Cornell Spe-*

cial *Educational Projects.* Ithaca, N.Y.: Committee on Special Educational Projects, undated (circa 1968 or early 1969).

Eckland, Bruce K., "Social Class and College Graduation: Some Misconceptions Corrected." *American Journal of Sociology,* Vol. 70, 1964a, pp. 36–50.

Eckland, Bruce K., "College Dropouts Who Came Back. *Harvard Educational Review,* Vol. 34, No. 3, 1964b, pp. 402–420.

Educational Testing Service, "Bias in Selection Tests and Criteria Studied by ETS and United States Civil Service." ETS *Developments,* Vol. 17, October 1969, p. 2.

Eells, Kenneth; Davis, Allison; Havighurst, Robert J.; Herrick, Virgil E.; and Tyler, Ralph W., *"Intelligence and Cultural Differences."* Chicago: University of Chicago Press, 1951.

Fishman, Joshua A.; Deutsch, Martin; Kogan, Leonard; North, Robert; and Whiteman, Martin, "Guidelines for Testing Minority Group Children." *Journal of Social Issues,* Vol. 20, 1964, pp. 127–145. (Supplement to the April issue, No. 2.)

Green, Robert Lee, and Farquhar, William W., "Negro Academic Motivation and Scholastic Achievement." *Journal of Educational Psychology,* Vol. 56, 1965, pp. 241–243.

Hills, John R., and Stanley, Julian C., "Prediction of Freshman Grades from SAT and from Level 4 of SCAT in Three Predominantly Negro State Colleges." *Proceedings of the 76th Annual Convention of the American Psychological Association,* 1968, pp. 241–242.

Hills, John R., and Stanley, Julian C., "Easier Test Improves Prediction of Black Students' College Grades. *Journal of Negro Education* (in press).

Humphreys, Lloyd G., "Racial Differences: Dilemma of College Admissions." *Science,* Vol. 166, October 10, 1969, p. 167. Letters section.

Jenkins, Martin D., *The Morgan State College Program—An Adventure in Higher Education.* Baltimore: Morgan State College Press, 1964. (For a review of this book emphasizing measurement aspects, see Julian C. Stanley, *Educational and Psychological Measurement,* Vol. 25, 1965, pp. 273–276.)

Jensen, Arthur R., "Selectivity of Minority Students in Higher Education." *Toledo Law Review,* 1970 (in press).

Joseph, Gloria, and Newsom, Barbara, "Cornell's Black Student: A Report from the Inside." *Cornell Alumni News,* June 1968.

Kendrick, S. A., "The Coming Segregation of Our Selective Colleges." *College Board Review,* No. 66, Winter 1967–68, pp. 6–13.

Kendrick, S. A., and Thomas, Charles L., "Transition from School to College." *Review of Educational Research,* Vol. 40, 1970, pp. 151–179.

Lee, Marilyn C., "Configural Versus Linear Prediction of College Academic Performance." Unpublished Ph.D. dissertation, University of Illinois, 1957. *Dissertation Abstracts,* Vol. 17, 1957, pp. 297–298.

Lennon, Roger T., *Testimony of Dr. Roger T. Lennon as Expert Witness on Psychological Testing in the Case of Hobson* et al. *vs. Hansen* et al. (*Washington, D.C., schools*). New York: Harcourt, Brace & World, 1968.

Lesser, Gerald S.; Fifer, Gordon; and Clark, D. H., "Mental Abilities of Children from Different Social-Class and Cultural Groups." *Monographs of the Society for Research in Child Development,* No. 30, 1965.

Ludlow, H. Glenn, "Some Recent Research on the Davis-Eells Games." *School and Society,* Vol. 84, 1956, pp. 146–148.

McPartland, James, "Should We Give Up School Desegregation?" *Johns Hopkins Magazine,* Vol. 21, April 1970, pp. 20–25.

Mitchell, Blythe C., "Predictive Validity of the Metropolitan Readiness Tests and the Murphy-Durrell Reading Readiness Analysis for White and for Negro Pupils." *Educational and Psychological Measurement,* Vol. 27, 1967, pp. 1047–1054.

Nicholson, Everard, *Success and Admission Criteria for Potentially Successful Risks.* Providence, R.I.: The author, Brown University.

Owen, John D., "Towards a More Consistent, Socially Relevant College Scholarships Policy." *Report No. 61,* Baltimore, Md.: Center for Social Organization of Schools, The Johns Hopkins University, January 1970.

Roberts, S. Oliver, and Oppenheim, Don B., "The Effect of Special Instruction upon Test Performance of High School Students in Tennessee." *Research Bulletin* RB-66-36. Princeton, N.J.: Educational Testing Service, July 1966, p. 9.

Ruch, Floyd L. Critical notes on "Seniority and testing under fair employment laws." *Industrial Psychologist,* Vol. 7, April 1970, pp. 13–25.

Sabine, Gordon A., "A Diary of Something About to Happen: Michigan State's Search for More Negro Students." *College Board Review,* No. 69, Fall 1968, pp. 11–14.

Somerville, Bill. "Can Selective Colleges Accommodate the Disadvantaged? Berkeley says 'Yes.'" *College Board Review,* No. 65, Fall 1967, pp. 5–10. For letters by Thomas W. Sutton and Julian C. Stanley concerning this article, and a reply by Mr. Somerville, see *College Board Review,* No. 66, Winter 1967–68, p. 39.

Stanley, Julian C., "Achievement by the Disadvantaged." *Science,* Vol. 163, February 14, 1969a, p. 622. Letters section.

Stanley, Julian C., "Confrontation at Cornell." *Trans-action,* Vol. 7, November 1969b, p. 54. Letters section.

Stanley, Julian C., "Plotting ANOVA Interactions for Ease of Visual Interpretation." *Educational and Psychological Measurement,* Vol. 29, 1969c, pp. 793–797.

Stanley, Julian C. "How Can We Intervene Massively?" *Science,* Vol. 167, January 9, 1970, p. 123. Letters section. Also see letters there and on p. 124 concerning Humphreys' letter by Alfred L. Baldwin and Harry Levin, Jerome Kirk, and Robert L. Williams.

Stanley, Julian C., and Porter, Andrew C., "Correlation of Scholastic Aptitude Test Scores with College Grades for Negroes versus Whites." *Journal of Educational Measurement,* Vol. 4, 1967, pp. 199–218.

Stodolsky, Susan B., and Lesser, Gerald S., "Learning Patterns in the Disadvantaged." *Harvard Educational Review,* Vol. 37, 1967, pp. 546–593.

Terman, Lewis M., and Oden, Melita, "The Gifted Child Grows Up." *Genetic Studies of Genius, IV.* Stanford, Calif.: Stanford University Press, 1947.

Tetlow, William L. Jr., "Academic Standards of COSEP." *Cornell Chronicle,* October 16, 1969, pp. 1, 6–7.

Thomas, Charles Leo, and Stanley, Julian C., "Effectiveness of High School Grades for Predicting College Grades of Black Students: A Review and Discussion." *Journal of Educational Measurement,* Vol. 6, 1969, pp. 203–215.

Wilson, Kenneth M., "Black Students Entering CRC Colleges: Their Characteristics and Their First-Year Academic Performance." *Research Memorandum 69-1.* Poughkeepsie, N.Y.: College Research Center, Vassar College, April 15, 1969.

Response to Julian C. Stanley's Paper

By Kenneth B. Clark

Professor Stanley does not directly answer the question posed in the title of his paper. A careful reading suggests that he believes that standardized test scores and high school grades are as effective in predicting success for disadvantaged students as they are for more privileged students, but all attempts to determine the empirical base on which this general feeling rests lead only to such general statements as, grades and test scores are rather potent predictors of continuation in school . . . probably we need more test information about the disadvantaged than about the advantaged . . . to expect good college grades from most students who have neither [good grades in high school and high test scores] is asking for a minor academic miracle. . . .

Presumably, all of the ideas brought together by Professor Stanley lead him to the conclusion that "aptitude test scores and high school grades, when used together, usually do predict college grades of disadvantaged applicants about as well as they do for regular ones," and the novel suggestion that "the more disadvantaged an applicant seems to be socioeconomically, the more objective information one needs about him."

If one analyzes and seeks to understand the point of view of Professor Stanley's paper, the dominant theme that emerges, and that is stated in a number of ways throughout his paper, is that Professor Stanley does not believe that special open admissions and compensatory educational programs are likely to be successful, even with massive educational remediation provided for the disadvantaged students at the college level. He is explicit in saying that these youngsters who have been educationally deprived throughout their elementary and secondary education will be unable to compete academically, will be frustrated, will resort to demands for "relevant" black studies programs that will be mere devices for avoiding more demanding curriculums, and probably will create difficulties and trouble in the colleges to which they will be admitted. Professor Stanley is pessimistic, if not fatalistic, about these programs. Throughout this pessimism there is the very strong suggestion that probably the only realistic way of dealing with education for the disadvantaged is through setting up for them segregated community and nonprestigious colleges. This argument is clearly against attempts on the part of prestigious colleges — more objectively defined as colleges with high academic standards — to opening their doors to the educationally disadvantaged.

I am personally concerned about the relationship between these ideas on the admissions policies of colleges and universities, which are largely ideas in defense of the status quo, and specific answers to the very important question raised in the title of Professor Stanley's paper. The question raised by him can either be answered by empirical evidence or not. Professor Stanley does not provide any adequate evidence concerning this question. The discussion of what type of higher education should be provided for disadvantaged students is a discussion of a policy matter. Of course, policy decisions of this sort must be backed up by the necessary program and procedural changes which will increase the chances of success. But Professor Stanley believes that such policy and procedural changes will not increase the chances of educating any substantial percentage of students on a single standard of college education. I disagree with him, and I believe that the evidence that will come from serious open admissions programs will support my point of view and refute Professor Stanley's.

Another disturbing thing about Professor Stanley's paper, and my comments about it, is that Professor Stanley and I have not defined, with any degree of precision, the term "disadvantaged." As one reads his paper it seems as if his concept of disadvantaged is a mixture of low scores and minority status. While he does not say that these are synonymous, the looseness of his paper certainly strongly suggests this. Maybe a more objective definition of disadvantaged students would be one that emphasizes elementary and secondary educational deprivation. With this approach to the nature of the disadvantaged student, it would seem to follow that effective programs for such students would meet the following requirements:

1. Select such students as demonstrate high motivation to continue in college as a way of overcoming earlier educational deficiencies;

2. Provide for such students the type of specialized compensatory and remedial education programs, with the necessary personnel, materials, and facilities to aid them in overcoming past educational deficiencies as quickly as possible;

3. Try to move them into a high standard of collegiate education as quickly as possible.

There is no reason to believe that a systematic program that provides the necessary resources in money, personnel, and commitment could not increase substantially the proportion of previously educationally disadvantaged youngsters in our colleges and help them to make constructive contributions to our society.

Finally, as colleges, prestigious or otherwise, embark on such serious programs, it will soon become clear that they will have to — with their influence and their educational power — raise the standards of elementary and secondary education in the public schools in order to prevent them from producing hundreds of thousands of educationally disadvantaged youngsters annually. If this were done, it would remove all bases of Professor Stanley's pessimism and, I would hope, provide him with other alternatives than educationally segregated postsecondary education for them.

Personal and Institutional Assessment: Alternatives to Tests of Scholastic Aptitude and Achievement in the Admissions Process

By Winton H. Manning

If the problem of access to higher education were simply that of assuring entrance to some college-level institution for every child who is interested in continuing his education beyond high school, it would be a formidable task, but there would be little reason for convening this conference as a means to bring about the attainment of this goal. Numbers of notable commissions and vast quantities of rhetoric have already been addressed to this question. It is a social and economic objective that will be solved primarily through the political process rather than through educational planning, however necessary the latter may be to the implementation of political decisions once they are made. Stated in unvarnished terms, universal access to higher education can probably be effected most directly by the upward extension of public higher education to grades 13 and 14 or beyond. Already this process is at work in many states, and although the economic and political obstacles to its full attainment are great, there is no reason to believe that with sufficient energy it cannot come about, as indeed it should.

Personally I am convinced that this is a desirable goal, not only because universal public higher education has a good potentiality for creating a richer, more satisfying life for our citizens but also because growing up in a technological, cybernetic society requires that we face squarely the necessity of constructing socially accessible alternatives to enforced idleness on the part of our youth. Certainly it is preferable to inventing new Vietnams, or to fostering the police state that would otherwise be needed to constrain the restless anger of legions of embittered, technologically unemployable, young adults.

Universal public education through grade 14 or beyond will not, however, fulfill adequately all the needs of society for advanced education, nor will it appropriately satisfy the legitimate aspirations of many young people. Despite its many shortcomings, one of the strengths of higher education in the United States is its diversity. Institutions of varying size, with different objectives and different environments offer the potentiality for nurturing a rich diversity of talent that must be valued in a democratic society. Heterogeneity of postsecondary educational opportunity, if it is to be maximally effective, also requires an admissions process through which students can distribute themselves rationally, and by which institutions can seek intelligently those students who will renew, in successive years, the particular role that the college seeks to play.

I assume, therefore, that the planners of this conference were, in addition to other aspects of the problem, concerned also with improving and expanding the measurement components of the admissions process.

In approaching this topic I was faced with a difficult choice. It is possible, for example, to discuss the problem of broadening the scope of measurement in admissions from the particular standpoint of providing better descriptions of *minority, disadvantaged young people* — a concern of various participants in this meeting including myself. Or, on the other hand, one could examine the problem from the perspective of making the system for distributing students more satisfying for all young people, rather than solely or especially for disadvantaged youth alone. I have chosen the more general approach to the problem for a number of reasons.

First, in this emotionally charged period of our history, I doubt very seriously the acceptability of solutions to the educational and social problems of poor Mexican American, black, and Puerto Rican children advanced by people who are not themselves members of one of these groups. More centrally, I believe that in the long run the solutions to educational problems of minority disadvantaged youth will have important consequences for bettering the lot of all young people and it will therefore be advantageous to consider the problem as broadly as we can. History contains many precedents which demonstrate that the strivings of oppressed peoples have resulted in social reorganizations that have benefited all persons in the society, not just those who were formerly members of the underclass. Among the most creative forces for reform in higher education in our time are the growing numbers of black and brown students who have not been content with what they found after gaining admission to "white" colleges. Whether it is the questions raised about the objectives and control of the college curriculum that have arisen in planning black studies programs, or whether it is in the movement for democratizing the governance of the institutions that has been initiated on many campuses by minority students, or whether it is in the revitalization of measurement research as a consequence of searching inquiries about cultural bias of tests taken by black students and other groups — in all these areas, the consequences of educational reform will be magnified far beyond the focus of concern of the particular group that initially triggered the search for improvement.

As a result, I have chosen to approach my assigned topic from a general perspective, partly as I have said out of strategic considerations, but primarily because I believe that behavioral science is most productive when problems are defined broadly, even though service applications deriving from research may well be directed to the particular needs of various groups.

The Need for Reform in the Admissions Process

The recent past has seen disruptive events of significance to the future vitality of higher education pile on top of one another and at such a pace that it can truly be said of the year just endured that there has been none other like it. However, in the midst of clamorous confrontations and bitter disillusionment at least one major, albeit scholarly, event in higher education has also occurred — namely, the publication by Feldman and Newcomb (1969) of a two-volume compendium of 40 years of research on colleges and their students. As reported in the *Journal of Higher Education* the report "summarizes research findings on how students are affected by the size and type of their college, by faculty members, by residential arrangements, by student cultures, by major fields of study, and by their own backgrounds and personalities. [It includes] . . . research on the persistence of change along with [. . . discussions of . . .] problems of interpretation, research tools, . . . research hazards . . . , and an exhaustive bibliography" (Anon., 1969, p. 228). This publication is, I believe, a landmark work that is deserving of careful study by those concerned with formulating educational policy at the college and university level.

It is also my impression, however, that this distinguished publication has attracted little attention except among the relatively small circle of scholars engaged in research on higher education. This is consistent with the singular state of affairs that exists with regard to policy formation in higher education, namely, that our institutions of higher learning have been relatively impervious to the products of social science research on higher education.

This indictment is not, I believe, greatly exaggerated, even though each of us can point to a few notable exceptions. It arises from a profound lack of fruitful relationships between educational research and policy making that has for many years characterized most of the important issues in human affairs more generally, with the possible exception of medicine. This is a melancholy assessment; I hope it is not a cynical one. It does, however, suggest the difficulty inherent in addressing the question of "how measurement of personality and other noncognitive traits can enlarge opportunity for higher education," which is another way of stating the assignment I was given for this conference. As will be seen later, I believe there are a number of ways that expanding the present domain, methods, and role of measurement in college admissions would, in combination with other more fundamental reforms, promote improved access of students to higher education. But the practical obstacles and historical precedents do not offer great encouragement to those who would like to see us rapidly bring about a more satisfying and equitable system for transition of students from secondary school to college. This is particularly so if one asks that the system also be grounded in solid, empirical research.

Put another way, I believe that two principal barriers to reforms in higher education are *ignorance* and *timidity.* That is, there is not yet in hand solid research evidence to support many of the desirable changes in our system of higher education that most would agree are important, and our researchers and university leaders are not yet sufficiently courageous or trusting to take the risks associated with instituting the purposeful system of cooperative educational experimentation that is desperately needed. Massive experimentation is desperately needed not only in the interest of extending educational opportunity to poor minority youth, but for all young people, if intelligent educational reforms are to occur.

Students are today more and more united in desperate concern, not only for their own survival but for the survival of their planet. Furthermore, they are now being joined in significant numbers by secondary school students, young adults out of college, and faculty members themselves. The purposes and beliefs that knit these often anguished groups of people together are vastly different from the scholarly ideals that have traditionally been enunciated by our universities, and in this confrontation of values it is not an exaggeration to state that the continued existence of some of our most renowned institutions of higher learning hangs in the balance.

The basis for distribution of students from high school to college constitutes a small but nevertheless important part of this larger problem—and the admissions process is one that is similarly in desperate need of reform. One idea that has long been proposed is that of broadening the domain of measurement employed in the admissions process. But this objective, as will be pointed out in later sections, cannot be expected to occur unless there is a comparable reform in the basic character of the process of transition, particularly the system of admission to college that is followed among selective institutions. But, first, let us consider the question of extending the range of student assessment to include other measures than those which have been traditionally employed.

Personality Measurement and College Selection

Writing several years ago, Samuel Messick provided a balanced and thoughtful analysis of the potential contributions of personality measurement in relation to college performance (Messick, 1964). As an introduction to the problem I could hardly do better than commend his paper to you for further study and attempt to summarize briefly the major points found therein.

The problem of assessing the role of personality measurement divides itself into two main questions — what is the scientific status of personality measurement, and what are the appropriate uses for such measures. Put more simply the first question is: "What do we now know?" The second is: "Knowing this, what do we want to do?"

From a scientific point of view, the assessment of personality is closely entwined with the problem of hypothesis testing and theory building in human psychological development. The adequacy of a particular measure of personality must in the long run be judged within the network of relationships that is shown to exist among the variables for which the theoretical constructs attempt to account. Since the status of personality theory is now at a fairly primitive level, there are many different approaches to the problem of personality measurement and, at best, the level of conceptual integration is at a relatively low status. Consequently, there does not now exist within the field a set of powerful, unifying, generally accepted constructs that can be operationally defined by particular sets of measurement instruments. In addition, the methodology of measurement poses particularly knotty problems in the field of personality testing. As compared with tests of aptitude and achievement, for example, personality measures are generally:

— less reliable,
— more inconsistent with respect to demonstrated validity for nontest performance,
— more subject to conscious and unconscious deception, faking, and malingering.
— less well integrated into theories of human development,
— more subject to arbitrary situational effects surrounding the context in which the measurements are made, and
— more likely to evoke feelings of anxiety, insecurity, or even hostility on the part of the person who is being assessed.

On the other hand, and herein lies perhaps much of their attraction,

— interpretations of personality measures are more likely to yield information of greater intrinsic personal interest to the individual being assessed than do tests of aptitude and achievement.

These observations are fairly general in their applicability but they do vary in their force, depending upon whether one is talking about self-report questionnaires, ratings of behavior by competent observers, or scores derived from objective performance tests. It is also true that significant advances have been made by researchers during the past decade, so that there are a number of promising new approaches to measurement of personality, particularly in areas that are concerned with the intersection of personality and cognition, or measures of cognitive style.

This cursory review of the scientific status of personality measurement would hardly be sufficient if it were not for the fact that the second of the two questions posed earlier — what are the *appropriate* uses of personality measures in college admissions — is overriding in its implications.

The question of appropriateness is, of course, another way of asking about the ethics and values that constitute the foundation of any socially acceptable system of measurement related to college selection. As Messick pointed out, "the choice of any particular personality measure for use, say, in college admission involves an implicit value judgment, which, at the least should be made explicit in an educational policy that justifies its use" (Messick, 1964, p. 840).

Making the policy explicit means as a minimum: (1) the selection of criteria of student performance that are presumed to be relevant and justifiable assessments of the outcome of the educational process; (2) the establishment of a consistent, stable, and significantly valid relationship between the personality measures and these criteria.

The crux of the problem is that the criterion should be no less subject to rigorous evaluation than are the predictors used as the basis for selection. Consequently if one finds that students with aggressive, authoritarian personalities make higher grades in an institution than do students displaying the polar opposites of these traits, what should be done?

Should more neofascist students be selected or should one seek to change the nature of the educational process so that a different relationship between predictor and the achievement criterion will exist? Presumably, in this instance it is the college that should change, not the selection process alone. Paul Heist's (1967) work showing that students identified as "creative" are more likely to drop out of college than others of equal ability illustrates the same problems of college selection very nicely.

A further deterrent to the use of personality measures in college admission as it is now practiced is inherent in the competitive nature of the admissions process. Any variable employed in the selection process, because of the intense personal interest that pervades the outcome of the decisions into which it enters, will come to acquire a regressive impact on students, thereby subtly influencing them to conform in those ways that they believe will be rewarded. Where social justification can be supplied, the use in selection of various measurement variables as a basis for rewards, thus encouraging growth in particular directions, may be desirable; however, these decisions should always be made with careful assessments of their social consequences. It is here that most observers would agree that the use of personality measures as bases for selection should be approached with great caution. Otherwise, we run the risk of rewarding particular behavioral styles, not because they are more useful to society, but because they happen to be predictive of some criterion of success in college however partial and inconclusive this index may be.

Guidance and Admissions Information Systems

I have indicated briefly some of the problems that seem on balance to diminish the attractiveness of personality measures as bases for college admission. However, this analysis was drawn almost wholly within the framework of the use of this type of information by *institutions* as alternatives or supplements to tests of achievement or ability in the process of selection. A somewhat different appraisal of personality measurement would be made if one were to look at the problem within a guidance context, and if the decisions were primarily those that are made by *students* in relation to their education and career decisions, rather than by institutions in relation to admissions decisions.

A realistic assessment of the future suggests that the nature of the transition from secondary school to college is changing in a number of fundamental ways. First, the populations being served are far more diverse than was true only a few years ago. Second, educational programs and organizational settings for learning are becoming even more greatly diversified, in response to these changes in population, and in recognition of the far greater diversity of institutional goals and student objectives. Thus the opportunities for choice by students are considerably enlarged. Finally, there are profound changes in the social needs and expectations of our society with regard to postsecondary education, and these basic changes in needs, values, and expectations have a potent influence on the kind of measurement information systems that must be developed for the future.

Measurement services for student and institutional decision-making may be broken down into three broad areas:
1. Systems for making decisions about *entry* into educational programs,
2. Systems for making decisions about the *process* of learning or instructional procedures within the course of an educational program, and
3. Systems for making decisions based upon evaluations of the *outcome* of educational programs.

Within each of these three phases, one may conceptualize a four-fold matrix of information exchange. On one axis are found the two sources of information: (a) systematic descriptions of the student, and (b) systematic descriptions of the educational programs of the institution. On the other axis are the two consumers of measurement services — (c) students and (d) institutions. Combining these in a two-by-two matrix yields four classes of measurement information services, each of which is pertinent to the three broad classes of decisions described above.

Guidance information services are concerned primarily with the provision of information to students about themselves and about institutions in connection with entry into educational programs. This information should be as broadly based as possible and should include measurement of as wide a range as possible of important and valid psychological and educational variables, including measures of interests, values, and personality, as well as measures of aptitude and achievement. Indeed, if the principal goals of guidance services are to assist students in gaining a more adequate perception of themselves and to provide an improved basis for their educational and career planning, including an understanding of the processes of decision-making, the collection of a broad range of descriptive student data is absolutely essential.

Admissions information services are by contrast concerned with the other two cells of the matrix referred to earlier — the systematic provision of information to institutions about themselves and about their potential or actual students for purposes of admission, placement, and financial aid.

As the Commission on Tests of the College Board has pointed out, there now exists a fundamental lack of symmetry in the four-fold matrix I have just described. On the whole, the kinds of information collected and disseminated by the College Board and other agencies are mainly concerned with the needs of institutions for information about students. Guidance information systems are designed only as secondary or derivative systems that capitalize somewhat adventitiously on the information that may be available. In particular, the measurement domains sampled are those that have traditionally been found useful to institutions for their selection needs rather than for the decision-making needs of the student, except insofar as the concerns of these two agents in the information exchange happen to intersect.

Writing some years ago, B. A. Thresher stated it well when he spoke of the transition into college as a "great sorting," that, as a social process, is not fully understood by students, parents, admissions officers, educators, or anyone else. Viewed as a whole, Thresher says this sorting process is "the product of an immense number of individual choices and decisions taken by millions of people, under the influence in part of calculations and estimates projected a generation into the future and in part of beliefs, opinions, whims, ancient loyalties, and areas of ignorance scarcely amenable to rational estimate'' (Thresher, 1966). If we are to develop guidance and admissions information systems that have as their goal the rationalizing of this sorting process, it seems evident that one must begin by devising systematic procedures and measurements that serve students and institutions equally well, and which are symmetrical in the sense that they are equally responsive to the needs of each party.

To the extent that educators try to develop more effective student-centered guidance information, they must turn correspondingly toward more complete descriptions of the individual in relation to educational opportunities. This means that information necessary to portray to the student his own personality traits, values, interests, experiences, aspirations, and aptitudes must somehow be assembled and systematically provided if we expect his choices and decisions to be intelligent. The paradox is that the present system, based as it is on identifying the most promising candidates for preferment within a hierarchical, meritocratic race for college, militates against the full disclosure of this kind of information by the student. Even if the methodological shortcomings I have described earlier could be overcome, serious concern would exist regarding the confidentiality of the data and possible invasions of privacy. Furthermore, assurances of great persuasiveness would need to be offered regarding the confidentiality of the data and the responsiveness of the system to the needs of the student if he is to participate on a voluntary rather than on a coercive basis. This will be difficult, but unless the fundamental character of the process of admission to college is changed, so as to remove or substantially reduce some of the iniquitous consequences of competition, the opportunity to develop truly effective guidance and admissions services will be vitiated, and student confidence will never be won.

Is it possible to purposefully design new and better systems for guidance and admission to college? I hope so, because there are increasing signs that the present system will not continue to be acceptable indefinitely, and at least some of the alternatives that may evolve will be, though different, no better. Perhaps they may be even more irrational than the "great sorting process" we now have, if that is possible.

Assessing the College as a Community of Learners

All knowledge is shared experience; its acquisition is an overwhelmingly social act. But the business of higher education is not primarily or exclusively concerned with the transmission of a cultural heritage of knowledge, as important as this may be. The provision of conditions that promote the development of the inner resources of the individual is equally important. The question of what should be the basis for admission to college is intimately related to the problem of creating the optimal conditions for assuring (1) the transmission of information from society to its novices, and (2) furthering the individuals' potential for self-development.

Of these two objectives, the first may be less dependent for its realization on the existence of a particular community of persons who contemporaneously share in the process of learning, while interacting together in a social group. Indeed, neither the movement toward independent study, nor the increasing automation of learning by means of computer assisted instruction would be possible unless this were not so.

The second objective, that of self-discovery and personal growth, depends in many ways upon the participation of the individual in a community of persons, who serve both as stimuli and as setting for this kind of learning and development. In practice, no single college community epitomizes in its environment either of these objectives. The task of information transmission is not simply that of an instructor coloring in the student's cognitive map; nor is the task of self-development pursued within the context of the university as a therapeutic agency.

Present admissions procedures are heavily weighted toward the first of these objectives, in that the use of high school record, and aptitude and achievement tests is predicated on the assumption that information transmission will be more optimally carried on if the community of learners is reduced to some degree in its variability. Furthermore, information transmission may be conceptually more closely allied to this aspect of individual differences, if one can generalize from some laboratory studies that are pertinent. This assumption is seriously questioned by some, and it is indeed difficult to specify experimental evidence that is directly relevant. Nevertheless, the substantial validity of cognitive ability measures for grade-average criteria seems consistent with this position.

At Educational Testing Service a study now in progress is pertinent to this question (Rock, 1970). In it the investigators are concerned with attempts to assess the differential impacts of colleges as they handle students of different ability levels. That is, the hypothesis is that certain colleges are more capable of showing significant gains for persons of relatively higher versus relatively lower ability levels. In the social studies area, preliminary results indicate that indices of selectivity, pragmatic orientation, high percent going to graduate school, size, and realistic orientation discriminate between colleges having differential effects in this regard. This suggests that particular types of colleges do a more effective job of fostering learning of some groups of students in the information transmission sense than they do for other groups. There may be some colleges, in other words, that are relatively more effective for lower than for higher ability students.

Are there colleges that foster personal and individual growth more effectively for some of their students than for others? Presumably there are, but the data are hard to find. Is it too much to ask that colleges and universities discover what they are doing well, and for whom, and that this information be available to students and others who need to know? That would truly be "college admission in the public interest."

The process of sorting students should, it seems to me, promote the formation of communities of learners that would represent a wide diversity of different environments for learning, and would nurture a broad range of personal and societal objectives. The question of formulating supplementary or alternative bases to achievement and ability measures is, therefore, most properly addressed as a need to respond to both of these two fundamental objectives of higher education — personal development as well as information transmission.

I believe this is what Edgar Friedenberg was also driving at when he urged the Commission on Tests to concern itself with the "fit" or congruence between students and institutions. He stated: "Education is shared experience, and only that, and the less continuity there is among those who share an educational institution, either between themselves or between their present and their past, the less profound and intense the educational experience is likely to be. There is, in short, something to be said for the educational use of tests that group together people who have enough in common to allow themselves to establish a community." (Friedenberg, 1970)

The principal promise of assessments of personality, in combination with tests of aptitude and achievement, seems to be in assisting students to seek and find learning environments that would foster personal self-development as an objective of higher education as worthy of attainment as that of the traditional goal of transmitting our heritage of knowledge. Guidance and admissions information systems that mediate student and institutional decisions within this expanded framework constitute a means for making the process of admission planful rather than irrational, and scientific rather than blind.

Inside the Input-Output Equation

In recent years we have seen substantial advances in our understanding of the differences among college environments. The work of Pace (1967), Stern (1962), Astin (1968), Holland (1958), Peterson (1965), Trow (1960), and others has led not only to increases in the quality of the research literature, but also to the development of such instruments as the College Student Questionnaire (1968), the College and University Environment Scales (1969), and the Institutional Functioning Inventory (1970), and to their dissemination through service programs that are designed to support institutional research. With sufficient effort we may confidently expect these instruments to be refined and expanded so that within this decade we should be able to provide reasonably sensitive and refined systems of services that are descriptive of institutional attributes and that will lend themselves to a useful taxonomy of learning environments at the higher education level.

Similarly, the assessment of personality, including both affective and cognitive domains already has reached levels of sophistication far ahead of the uses of such measurement procedures in college admissions. Assessment of student input and output characteristics, broadly defined, now constitutes the focus of several large research projects in this country and abroad. The methodological problems, though complex, seem either to have yielded to analysis by statistical theorists, or they offer promise of doing so. New information handling techniques and related applications of computer technology now afford the means for longitudinal data storage and retrieval that only a few years ago constituted significant barriers to large, comprehensive studies of student change.

What is not yet understood is how student characteristics interact with learning environments to produce different outcomes. This is, on a large scale, the aptitude-by-treatment interaction problem most recently addressed by Cronbach and Snow (1969). Put another way, the problem is that a good deal is known about inputs, both institutional and individual; some things are known about outputs, but very little is known about what is going on inside the systems equation.

This state of affairs is characteristic of another area that is presently being subjected to searching review, namely, the problem of evaluating the effectiveness of compensatory programs in early childhood education. Campbell and Erlebacher (1970) have pointed out the inadequacy of many of the experimental designs that have been employed in recent evaluations of programs such as Head Start, and have persuasively called for a revision in priorities by administrators, legislators, and others responsible for implementing educational policy. In particular, Campbell points out the need for an "experimenting society" (Haworth, 1960; Campbell, 1969) which would undertake massive studies that would desirably employ random assignment of subjects to treatments rather than post hoc matching designs for the purpose of evaluating the impact of these new educational programs. The employment of randomized experimental designs has great methodological attractiveness, and its merits are ably cataloged by Campbell and Erlebacher (1970).

Randomization does indeed offer not only methodological advantages, but it is also an attractive means for studying in genuine experiments the inter-action of student and environmental characteristics. Furthermore, the strategy of randomization may lead to more pervasive reforms in the admissions proc-ess itself. In this respect I am not arguing for the kind of random assignment of students that I understand Thresher (1966) and Astin (1970) to have sug-gested. I take their suggestions to represent random assignment as a solution to a frightful dilemma, or as the best of a number of possibly bad solutions. What I am proposing is simply the undertaking of a cooperative venture on the part of a substantial number of colleges and universities in which a given pro-portion of their students would be admitted to each participating institution from a previously constituted pool of "experimental" subjects. This body of students would provide a vehicle for a massive longitudinal inquiry that would lead to a number of specific possible outcomes, including the provision of the founda-tion for a guidance and admissions information system that would be coopera-tive rather than competitive in its essential functioning, and which would there-fore move us away from the competitive race that now characterizes the ad-missions process.

The Proposal in Brief

Let me briefly sketch the outline of the proposal that I have in mind:

(1) We should begin by securing the cooperation of a sample of colleges and universities that are willing to join together in creating a council of experi-menting institutions. For purposes of discussion, these should be about 80 in number, and they should be reasonably representative of the diversity of higher education institutions in the United States. A larger number would be even more desirable. In order to simplify this idea, I will call this "new" College Board the ACORN '80, in deference to the logotype that has for some years adorned College Board publications. For those who are more inclined to the fashion of acronyms, the name can be amplified as signifying an "Associational Council on Research Needs for the '80's."[1]

Each of these institutions must, of necessity, have several characteristics, including: a commitment to scientific, rational evaluation; the resources to mount intensive compensatory programs; the vitality to maintain a commitment to experimentation by faculty, students, administrators, and the surrounding community; and the courage to abandon for a significant proportion of its enter-

---

1. Elsewhere I have discussed the idea of ACORN '80 in terms of a consortium for experimentation on a wide range of educational problems. There is no implication that results of this experimentation would not be implemented until 1980; rather, it is proposed that the 1970s should be a period of inten-sive experimentation and innovative action designed to meet the present and future demands upon higher education.

ing class the use of any selection procedures whatsoever. (A minimum of 10 percent of the entering class randomly assigned is desirable, and a maximum of 20 percent should probably not be exceeded.) Assuming that about 50 of these 80 colleges have the fortitude and good luck to maintain their participation over two years, perhaps 10,000 or more students would be enrolled and followed in this program.

(2) A pool of students should be defined from among a population of those students whose financial need is sufficiently great as to require, on the average, aid in an amount equal or exceeding in absolute amounts at least 50 percent of the costs of attending the more expensive of the ACORN '80 colleges. Furthermore, they might receive at least that amount, wherever they may be assigned. This is obviously an arbitrary cutoff that is designed to make students interested in volunteering for participation in this project. In practice, the population of ninth- or tenth-grade students would be circularized with respect to the opportunity afforded by this new approach to admissions, and from among these a number would be randomly selected into the applicant pool. This pool would be sufficiently large to yield a number that could be accommodated within the aggregate of reserved places among the ACORN '80 colleges. Gauging the financial need criterion appropriately should also permit ample variation of aptitude and personality traits to occur, despite some restriction in socioeconomic class that is inevitable if this becomes the principal variable defining the applicant pool.

The students who are selected would be given absolute assurance of college admission to one of the ACORN '80 colleges, with a full allowance of financial aid. As such, they would represent an experiment in *guaranteed access to higher education* that is comparable to the guaranteed income experiment. This may have interesting consequences in its own right, and represents an important concept.

(3) During the tenth, eleventh, and twelfth grades, each student would complete an extensive array of assessment instruments, which would be designed to systematically portray his strengths, weaknesses, preferences, and plans. Each student would also need to be counseled throughout this entire period, and every effort would be expended to maintain participation even if it appeared that his immediate postsecondary educational plans might be seriously jeopardized by assignment to certain of the colleges. By this means, each student would be encouraged to stay in the project even if this meant postponing entry into an unavailable program that he would otherwise consider. This is essential if genuine randomization is to be maintained.

(4) Students would in due course be assigned at random to each of the cooperating institutions and within each of these to an "experimental" or "regu-

lar'' treatment. This represents the toughest task of all, since it requires that one see as Campbell states that . . . ''the number of persons so treated within . . . the experiment has not increased the number so deprived, but has instead reassigned some of that deprivation so that the ethical value of knowing may be realized . . . . Is randomization as the mode of such reassignment ethically defensible? It might represent an ethical cost (one nonetheless probably worth paying) if all children in the nation had been rank ordered on need, and those most needy given the compensatory education up to the budgetary and staff limits of the program. But, instead, the contrast is with a very haphazard and partially arbitrary process that contains unjust inversions of order of need far more extensive than a randomization experiment involving a few thousand children would entail. These unjust deprivations are normally not forced to our attention, and so do not trouble our ethical sensitivities as does the deprivation of the control group. But there is no genuine ethical contrast here'' (Campbell, 1970, p. 26).

(5) The outcomes of the experiment would be threefold: (a) A comparison of experimental and control groups, replicated across a number of college environments would provide valuable evidence concerning the efficacy of experimental programs (particularly, if several model programs were cooperatively designed) and would provide evidence for assigning subjects to different treatments, if they should prove effective. (b) For the control groups a study of the success and satisfaction of students, using criteria reflecting both information transmission and personal development objectives, would in relation to variations in college environments provide a significant forward step toward filling in the ''inside'' of the input-output equation. In time this would also provide a basis for developing, through iterations of this procedure for several cohorts, the linkage between personal and environmental characteristics that is needed for full realization of a guidance and admissions information system. (c) The results would provide a basis for establishing whether colleges do have different impacts, something that has been claimed but not really examined experimentally. In time this could lead to a systematic program of institutional evaluation.

A number of other interesting problems could also be addressed within the framework of such a study. For example, a sample of students could be selected who would not matriculate in any one of the ACORN '80 colleges but would rather pursue their college work independently, leading to encouragement for institutionally unaffiliated students to work toward an independent degree, should this in the future become a possibility.

It would also be necessary to provide counseling and financial assistance for students who at the end of their first year wished to transfer to another institution, or who had demonstrated fairly conclusively that they were either bored by the lack of challenge in the college to which they were originally assigned, or unable to withstand the rigors of its academic requirements.

There are many other details about which it would be tempting to speculate, including the possible cost of such a venture. This is difficult to estimate, but is unlikely to run more than $10 million for a peak year, for a total of perhaps $20 million over the five-year span of the project, including the cost of the financial aid awards to the students. This is not a large price in view of the fact that some compensatory programs are now costing in the vicinity of $1 thousand per student per year, and this amount does not ordinarily include the costs of recruiting the students into the program.

"After the Ball Is Over . . . ."

There is every reason to believe that a project such as the one just described would not, in fact, come to a definitive end. On the contrary, one would hope that "after the ball was over . . ." the party would truly begin. That is, by studying several successive waves of students it would become possible to move systematically from random assignment to an assignment of students based upon an intelligent, planful capitalization on the congruence of personal and institutional characteristics. Lest I be mistaken, I am not talking about "docile" students attending "pastoral" colleges, but rather the intention is to devise a prescriptive use of student and institutional assessments so as to maximize the likelihood of "successful" outcomes. Nor would the system necessarily be mechanistically external to the student's own expressed choices regarding institutions. Rather, a genuine clearinghouse, or probably several overlapping clearinghouses, could result in which measurement would serve as a vehicle for enhancing the value of the transition process to students and institutions alike.

Elijah Jordan (1952) has characterized the problem of mediating between the private interest of colleges and the public interest of social scientists when he said of the legislative process that institutions are blind but powerful, whereas the individuals have vision but are weak. The purpose of developing a renewed commitment to genuine educational experimentation is to provide a union between these two forces. Each without the infusion of the other becomes something less than it might be. Certainly there is much in higher education today that is evocative of the myth of blind Sisyphus, condemned endlessly to toil up the mountainside only to fail at the last. And, of all the indictments of social science, including psychological measurement, that of ingenious, visionary pursuit of the gutless problem is perhaps the most telling.

Alternatives to tests of aptitude and achievement in the admissions process are not likely to be found in tests of other less obvious, more exotic, undeveloped abilities. Rather, these alternatives arise when one is prepared to recognize that ignorance and timidity are still the principal obstacles to human progress.

The reality of individual differences is troublesome to many persons, particularly when they seem to get in the way of the social objective of eliminating barriers to higher education. But the alternative of denying their existence is even more unappealing. In this respect, I was struck recently by a passage in Kurt Vonnegut's powerful memoir, *Slaughterhouse-Five,* where he says: "I think about my education sometimes. I went to the University of Chicago for a while after the Second World War. I was a student in the Department of Anthropology. At that time, they were teaching that there was absolutely no difference between anybody. They may be teaching that still. . . . Another thing they taught was that nobody was ridiculous or bad or disgusting. Shortly before my father died he said to me, 'You know, you never wrote a story with a villain in it.' I told him that was one of the things I learned in college after the war." (Vonnegut, 1969)

The alternative to what we are doing now in the college admissions process is not to deny the existence of human or institutional variability, but rather for higher education to make a genuine commitment to rest its educational policies on the best evidence that behavioral science can offer, and to resolutely reform its procedures so as to maximize dependence upon what is empirically shown to be effective. To do this requires the courage that is implicit in a willingness to incur the risks that experimentation demands. The admissions barrier is perhaps from this perspective a "paper tiger." It exists primarily because of a lack of genuine experimentation; it is in reality a special case of the resistance to innovation in education that many have deplored in recent years and which is responsible for the sterility and emptiness that many students say is characteristic of their college experience. As such dedication to the time-honored solutions of the past are good examples of what F. Scott Fitzgerald was talking about when he said: "The strongest guard is placed at the gateway to nothing . . . maybe because the condition of emptiness is too shameful to be divulged" (Fitzgerald, 1934).

References

Anonymous, "The Research Gap." *Journal of Higher Education,* Vol. *41,* 1970, pp. 228–232.

Astin, A. W., *The College Environment.* Washington, D.C.: American Council on Education, 1968.

Astin, A. W., "Should College Applicants Be Selected by Lottery?" *Science,* Vol. 167, 1970, pp. 1075–1076.

Campbell, D., "Reforms as Experiments." *American Psychologist,* Vol. *24,* 1969, pp. 409–429.

Campbell, D., and Erlebacher, A., *How Regression Artifacts in Quasi-experimental Evaluations Can Mistakenly Make Compensatory Education Look Harmful.* May 1, 1970. Mimeographed.

College and University Environment Scales, Technical Manual, Second Edition. Princeton, N.J.: Educational Testing Service, 1969.

College Student Questionnaire, Technical Manual (Rev. 1968). Princeton, N.J.: Educational Testing Service, 1968.

Cronbach, L. J., and Snow, R., *Individual Differences in Learning Ability as a Function of Instructional Variables.* Final Report, U.S. Office of Education, Contract No. OEC 4-6-061269-1217. Stanford, Calif.: Stanford University, School of Education, March 1969.

Feldman, K. A., and Newcomb, T., *The Impact of College on Students.* 2 vols. San Francisco: Jossey-Bass, 1969.

Fitzgerald, F. S., *Tender Is the Night.* New York: Charles Scribner's Sons, 1934.

Friedenberg, E., *Can Testing Contribute to the Quest for Community Among Students.* 1970. Mimeographed.

Haworth, L., The Experimental Society: Dewey and Jordan. *Ethics,* Vol. 71, 1960, pp. 27–40.

Heist, P., "Creative Students: College Transients," in Paul Heist (ed.), *Education for Creativity: A Modern Myth.* Berkeley, Calif.: Center for Research and Development in Higher Education, 1967, pp. 21–48.

Holland, J. L., "Student Explanations of College Choice and Their Relationship to College Popularity, College Productivity, and Sex Differences." *College and University,* Vol. 33, 1958, pp. 313–320.

Institutional Functioning Inventory, Technical Manual. Princeton, N.J.: Educational Testing Service (in press), 1970.

Jordan, E., *Theory of Legislation.* (2nd ed.) Chicago: University of Chicago Press, 1952.

Messick, S., "Personality Measurement and College Performance," in Messick, S., and Jackson, D. N. (eds.) *Problems in Human Assessment.* New York: McGraw-Hill, 1967, pp. 834–845.

Pace, C. R., *Analyses of a National Sample of College Environments.* Final Report of USOE Contract No. 5-0764. June 1967.

Peterson, R., "On a Typology of College Students." *Research Bulletin* RB-65-9. Princeton, N.J.: Educational Testing Service, 1965.

Rock, D., *Personal communication.*

Stern, G. G., "Environments for Learning," in Nevitt Sanford (ed.) *The American College.* New York: John Wiley and Sons, 1962.

Thresher, B. A., *College Admissions and the Public Interest.* New York: College Entrance Examination Board, 1966.

Trow, M., "The Campus Viewed as a Culture," in H. T. Sprague (ed.), *Research on College Students.* Boulder, Colo.: The Western Interstate Commission for Higher Education; and Berkeley, Calif.: The Center for Higher Education, 1960, pp. 105–123.

Vonnegut, K. Jr., *Slaughterhouse-Five.* New York: Dell, 1969.

Response to Winton H. Manning's Paper

By Hugh W. Lane

"When you notice a cat in profound meditation,
  The reason, I tell you, is always the same:
His mind is engaged in a rapt contemplation
  Of the thought, of the thought, of the thought of his name:
    His ineffable effable
    Effanineffable
Deep and inscrutable singular Name."   *T. S. Eliot*

Fits and Starts

I could, of course, talk about the National Scholarship Service and Fund for Negro Students (NSSFNS), and describe our modest attempts to develop alternatives to tests of scholastic aptitude and achievement in the admissions process. I will not. The NSSFNS staff will present a panel at the Annual Meeting of the National Association of College Admissions Counselors (Boston, Massachusetts, September 30-October 3, 1970) which goes into the details of our new system. Much of the new system mirrors what may be the thinking of David Tiedeman and what we understand to be the thinking of Lee Cronbach. My paper today is not essentially concerned with NSSFNS or with the black issue. True, black *is* propaedeutic and all that that means — stated even better by Winton Manning — but my comment, like his paper, tries to deal with the American educational scene. It is, I hope, consistent with blackness, but that is not my purpose here.

A recent letter to the editors of *Science* notes the cost of the aborted flight of Apollo 13 to be $380 million and labels it the most expensive legal abortion in history. The writer then compares that cost with the $400 million annual budget of the National Science Foundation, making the point that our real national priorities are directly represented in the way funds are allocated and monies are spent.

Elsewhere I noticed the cost of each Phantom jet aircraft equipped for combat to be on the order of $2½ million. It struck me immediately that this cost was exactly half the total federal budget for Educational Talent Search. Thus Educational Talent Search is evaluated via the budgetary process as being worth two Phantom aircraft; Special Services with an annual allocation of $10 million is equated to the value of four Phantom jets.

Clearly other more telling comparisons could be found suggesting the conclusion that behind the rhetoric and the promises we do not place a very high value on the higher learning for minority/poverty students.

Higher education itself is grossly underfunded. This is the only conclusion one can reach after reading the various excellent reports of the Carnegie Corporation sponsored Commission on Higher Education, and noting the discrepancy between funding proposals for higher education and the funding levels actually attained from year to year.

The present picture, then, is one of the financing of higher education for minority/poverty students, grossly underfunded, considered within the context of higher education, itself grossly underfunded, while billions are spent on Vietnam, trips to and from the moon, and so forth. Thus considerations of priorities are presented to us as considerations of resources.

The argument here is that the very language of *selection* and *admission* assume real prior restrictions and limitations on resources that do not necessarily exist.

Suppose for a moment that they do not exist and that we have enough money to educate the American people. It then would become apparent that higher education is operated from a viewpoint of scarcity of resources when the real problem is that higher education is low on the scale of American priorities. Certainly it is relatively low when direct comparisons are made with the level of spending in selected other areas. Certainly it is relatively low when compared with estimates of the cost to be incurred if all the American people of the college age and grade class were to be educated.

Of course not all Americans share a commitment to higher learning as appropriate for all Americans. Vice president Agnew's remarks — reprinted in the spring issue of the *College Board Review* — make it clear that he does not share this goal. "I do not," he writes, "accept the proposition that every American boy and girl should go to a four-year college." He then goes on to endorse the position taken by no less a person than Amitai Etzioni, of Columbia University, in a letter written recently to the *Wall Street Journal*, to wit: ". . . If we can no longer keep the flood gates closed at the admissions office, it at least seems wise to channel the general flow away from four-year colleges and toward two-year extensions of high school in the junior and community colleges." This last seems to suggest a dubious future for the junior and community colleges, separate and apart from the traditions of the higher learning.

Let me argue for a moment that higher education receives all the support it warrants from those who set our national priorities. From their point of view it may really be the province of a "natural aristocracy" — Agnew quoting Thomas Jefferson — "a privilege," not "a right." Within this context, the function of admissions — and tests of scholastic aptitude and previous achievement — is to control the gates lest they become flood gates (Etzioni), lest the natural aristocracy within be inundated (Agnew).

Indeed a similar statement might be made about tuition. A subway-card ad in New York City notes that one-third of the costs of attending college is paid through tuition. As two-thirds thus comes from elsewhere, tuition can be seen as a "means test" determining who and which will be allowed to participate in the "value added" which is the higher learning, which is made possible by contributions, endowment, and the tax dollar.

Tests of scholastic aptitude used in the admissions process allow some students through the gates; they keep others out. The scholarship industry provides a kind of protective cover that says the game is fair — that it is not socio-economically biased.

Tests of scholastic aptitude tell some students that they are unworthy of entering the gate. Humphrey Doermann's tables show with stark clarity just how many are so deemed and how the effect is multiplied to the disadvantage of the poor as a function of the high intercorrelation of family income and test performance.

Indeed Doermann really lets the cat (whose Name I seek) out of the bag when he, in a single paragraph, notes that the median score of those taking the Scholastic Aptitude Test each year is roughly 500 and then two sentences later says that of all United States male high school graduates about 25 percent could score 450 or better on the verbal sections.

Now he is certainly not naive. He simply knows that the scale was first fixed in 1941 over a limited set of students mostly from the Northeastern seaboard. Thus our "continual reference point" turns out to be a fairly sophisticated elite.

Stimulated, piqued, and intrigued by Doermann's paragraph, I searched for and found *College Board Score Reports, 1969–70.* From it I produced Table 1, which could be entitled "Proportion Scoring Above and Below the Median (500) on the SAT."

I am suggesting that as long as we hold to such an elitist reference point in reporting test scores to students, their teachers, and their parents, we are — the College Board and Educational Testing Service (ETS) — telling usually well over 50 percent of the American student body that they do not measure up to scratch. Indeed the proportion falling below the median rises as high as 84 percent of girls rated on Mathematics while they are juniors in high school.

Now I know that both *College Board Score Reports* (1969-70), which goes to counselors and admissions officers, and *Your College Board Scores* (1969) which goes to students, include percentile ranks and actual mean scores, but the mean is assumed by all but the most sophisticated to be 500. And "*thus* the native hue of resolution is sicklied o'er with the pale cast of thought; and enterprises of great pith and moment, with this regard, their currents turn awry, and lose the name of action . . . ."

Table 1. Proportion Scoring Above and Below the Median (500)* on the SAT

	Boys		Girls	
	V	M	V	M
All juniors, national sample, fall 1966	18	27	18	16
	(82)	(73)	(82)	(84)
All juniors who took the SAT, May 1968 through March 1969	39	57	40	42
	(61)	(43)	(60)	(58)
All juniors in the 1966 national sample who later entered college	27	52	37	38
	(73)	(48)	(64)	(62)
All seniors who took the SAT, May 1968 through March 1969	35	54	37	37
	(65)	(46)	(63)	(63)
All seniors in the 1966 national sample who later entered college	30	56	41	38
	(70)	(44)	(59)	(62)

Note: Percentages in parentheses are those whose scores are below 500.

*Editor's note: The author's use of the term, "the median (500)," here refers to his citation of Doermann's statement that this is roughly the median score of those who take the SAT each year. Readers may be interested to know that the actual median verbal and mathematical scores of all who took the SAT from July 1969 through May 1970 were, respectively, 454 and 485. These are approximately the same as the medians for the past several years but do not alter or refute the central point illustrated by the author's table.

Is it possible that I am saying that the actual societal function of tests, of the College Board and ETS, may be to tell most students that they do not measure up to par? I guess I am.

Benjamin Bloom (1968), interestingly enough, and John Carroll (1963) have taken a different tack. Taking the aptitude distribution as a point of departure, Bloom notes at the top of the distribution some 5 percent of students likely to have some special talent for a subject. At the other extreme he notes some 5 percent with probable special disabilities for the particular learning. "In between are approximately 90 percent of the individuals where we believe (as does Carroll) that aptitudes are predictive of rate of learning rather than the level (or complexity) of learning that is possible. Thus, we are expressing the view that, given sufficient time (and appropriate types of help), 95 percent can learn a subject up to a high level of mastery. We are convinced that the grade of A as an index of mastery of a subject can, under appropriate conditions, be achieved by up to 95 percent of the students in a class.'' Bloom's paper and Carroll's earlier one will reward careful reading.

If one can reason from actual expenditures on higher education to the conclusion that only some top strata of students are to be educated and from this assumption see the real role played by admissions and financial aid, then the present forms that testing takes and the present effects of testing should have been predictable.

If, however, one reasons with Bloom and Carroll that aptitude is the amount of time required by the learner to attain mastery of a learning task and that 95 percent of the people can be brought to mastery in any particular learning task then indeed the whole notion of admissions disappears. If all can be educated, then there is no function of admissions. If admissions remains, then its function is rationing, not education.

Some hold the theory that the American experiment in democracy assumes a literate electorate. Each is to be educated to the level of mastery because the success of the experiment depends upon it. This seems to suggest that we are supposed to *develop* talent that exists in every citizen, not to *identify* talent that exists in only a few.

Bloom and Carroll proceed to identify the parameters that enter the equation of learning. They involve: ''. . . five elements — three residing in the individual and two stemming from external conditions. Factors in the individual are (1) aptitude — the amount of time needed to learn the task under optimal instructional conditions, (2) ability to understand instruction, and (3) perseverance —the amount of time the learner is willing to engage actively in learning. Factors in external conditions are (4) opportunity—time allowed for learning, and (5) the quality of instruction — a measure of the degree to which instruction is presented so that it will not require additional time for mastery beyond that required in view of aptitude'' (Carroll, 1963).

Carroll's full discussion deserves careful reading and rereading. Bloom's elaboration should be memorized.

Let me suggest some of the forms that emerge as we broaden ''the circle of our psychometric understanding'' (Manning, 1968).

Sally Counts (1952) used Thurstone's Test of Primary Mental Abilities on students and faculty in a study seeking patterns of success and failure in the learning of college mathematics.

She was able to demonstrate several patterns of the primary mental abilities residing in students receiving A's in the course and different patterns in students who received D's and F's. These patterns were not reducible to verbal and mathematical ability as represented in the Scholastic Aptitude Test but are more basic and less oriented toward school or college content. She demonstrates that there is more than one road to mastery—more than one combination of abilities that enables different people to master the same content with a differing combination of skills. Many of her related hypotheses are not borne out by the data, but her work suggests what testing *could* become.

In this connection, I have never fully understood why the Educational Testing Service named a building after Louis Thurstone, for the reduction of the person parameters seen by Thurstone as descriptive of learning potential to essentially two—verbal and mathematical—strikes an arc against the soul and meaning of Thurstone's life work.

Ginther and Rippey (Rippey, 1969) suggest in a parallel fashion that in teaching and learning there are pupil parameters, teacher parameters, parameters inherent in the teaching materials, and parameters in the approach to programing or pedagogy. The Ginther model is pretty heavy stuff at times, but the suggestion that emerges as appropriate for this discussion is that *testing* must be related to some conceptual model for learning itself. The results of testing must be meaningful statements about the behaviors of the person being tested, relevant to the situation or situations in which his behavior is expected to change in desired directions. Such testing would indeed be both diagnostic and prescriptive.

It is clearly not necessary that tests be an actual barrier to access to higher education. Higher education could be available to all students who complete a secondary education. Tests should not be barriers at all. Winton Manning (1968) has already called for "developing measurement instruments for prescriptive and educative functions." He has pointed out the difficulties, but as for defining the ground ahead, he has been right on.

In his paper he calls for ACORN '80, a sort of mass experimental college or set of experimental colleges. I laud his proposal without necessarily endorsing his details. The notion is correct. I am bothered by his apostrophe. He initially derives the 80 from the number of colleges to be involved, saying there should be about 80 or so. A little later he invents an acronym and calls it an "Associational Council on Research Needs for the '80s." The apostrophe apparently stands in lieu of 1900. We can't wait 10 more years.

If ACORN '80 is a substitute for the present thrust toward equal access to existing institutions, then it will cause diffusion of effort and be a barrier itself. I trust his motivation, but not that of all who might take an advocacy position vis à vis his proposal.

Emile Durkheim (1947) described two differing kinds or levels of social organization. He called them *mechanical* solidarity and *organic* solidarity. To the extent that a society is mechanically solidar, the parts—people, not persons — are interchangeable. "Kill a mule, buy another one . . . ." As a society becomes organically solidar, the concept of the person or the individual emerges. Individuals become important in the sense that the separate organs of the body are not interchangeable. When an organ dies, the body loses its viability and integrity.

Societies progress from mechanical toward organic solidarity. However, vestiges of each mode of solidarity exist side by side and contemporaneously.

I would argue that our educational institutions show this same characteristic progression. In the fashion of the mechanically solidar we educate each for all. The lecture, the common reader or textbook, the fixed curriculum, the system of pass–fail, indeed the notion of universal education to some least common denominator of performance assume interchangeable units. The notion of centrally administered common tests arises from a conception that society is mechanically solidar.

From this common base, however, we recognize the emergence of the individual. Elective courses, quality letter grades, advanced placement, specialization, diagnostic scoring — all and each of these involve a recognition of individual differences, different paths to mastery even to the point of individual one-to-one instruction, even to the point of independent study, and give evidence of organic solidarity as the basis for these institutional arrangements.

The forum for an early discussion of the issues involved in the choice between clinical and actuarial prediction was the 1955 Invitational Conference of Educational Testing Service. Paul Meehl, Nevitt Sanford, and others participated. Actuarial prediction, in my view, is basically mechanical though it shows some persons emerging in organic solidarity. Clinical prediction assumes each is organically related to the other and to the society. Actuarial prediction is both less expensive and more reliable. We still await, however, the day when actuarial forms provide the kind of clinical evidence upon which to base action in advising and teaching the individual student.

The George G. Stern book, *People in Context,* has recently been published. The subtitle is *Measuring Person-Environment Congruence in Education and Industry.* Its relevance to the subject under present discussion is evident. I will quote only from the last chapter, entitled "The Test: Trial or Tool," which begins with a quote from Alexander Pope.

"Know then thyself, presume not God to scan;
The proper study of mankind is man.
Placed on this isthmus of a middle state,
A being darkly wise, and rudely great:
With too much knowledge for the sceptic side,
With too much weakness for the stoic's pride."

It ends with a hopeful and apt paragraph, "But the need to apply restrictions at the initial point of college entrance is growing less and less. We are within sight of the day when anyone will be able to go to school for as long as he is able to demonstrate mastery of some subject matter being taught in some type of institution in which he has an interest. When educational opportunity is the same for all, tests become a tool rather than a trial. It becomes increasingly important to know where one's interests really lie. Tests will be used by the respondent in a spirit of self-discovery, as an aid in his search to identify and develop his own unique talents. They have been used in this way for many years, although not to the extent that they will be before this century is over . . ."

Testing, itself, must reflect the emergence of the division of labor. When "the circle of our psychometric understanding" is so enlarged we will have discovered the cat's "ineffable effable effanineffable deep and inscrutable singular Name."

"A Cat's entitled to expect
These evidences of respect,
And so in time you reach your aim,
And finally call him by his NAME.

So this is this and that is that:
And there's how you AD-DRESS A CAT."   *T. S. Eliot*

References

Bloom, Benjamin S., "Learning for Mastery." *Evaluation Comment,* UCLA Center for the Study of Instructional Programs, Vol. 1, No. 2, May 1968.

Carroll, John B., "A Model of School Learning." *Teachers College Record,* Vol. 64, No. 8., May 1963.

Counts, Sarah, "Achievement in College Mathematics as a Function of Instructors' and Students' Patterns of Primary Mental Abilities." Unpublished doctoral dissertation. University of Chicago, 1952.

Cronbach, Lee J., "Can a Machine *Fit* an Applicant to Continuing Education?" *Measurement and Evaluation in Guidance,* Vol. 2, No. 2, Summer 1969.

Durkheim, Emile, *Division of Labor in Society.* Glencoe, Ill.: Free Press, 1947.

Eliot, T. S., *Old Possum's Book of Practical Cats.* New York: Harcourt, Brace and Company, 1939. The quotation on page 100 is from "The Naming of Cats." The quotation on page 107 is from "The Ad-dressing of Cats."

Manning, Winton H., "The Measurement of Intellectual Capacity and Performance," *The Journal of Negro Education,* Vol. XXXVII, No. 3, Summer 1968, pp. 258–267.

Meehl, Paul E., et al., "Clinical vs. Actuarial Prediction." In a panel discussion. Proceedings: 1955 Invitational Conference on Testing Problems, pp. 93–141. Princeton, N.J.: Educational Testing Service.

Rippey, Robert M., "The Ginther Model: Four Dimensions of Research on Instruction." *The Elementary School Journal,* Vol. 69, No. 4, January 1969.

Stern, George G., *People in Context.* New York: John Wiley & Sons, Inc., 1970.

Tiedeman, David V., "Can a Machine Admit an Applicant to Continuing Education?" *Measurement and Evaluation in Guidance,* Vol. 2, No. 2, Summer 1969.

Programs and Practices
for Minority Group Youth in Higher Education

By Edmund W. Gordon

In the past 10 years a great deal of publicity and attention has been given to efforts at offering expanded opportunities for higher education to members of minority groups or other disadvantaged populations. This recent movement, however, is not the first time that the attention of educators has been directed at this goal. There were some few black students in higher education even before the Civil War, and the postwar period of reconstruction included a concerted effort at making available postsecondary education for minority groups, especially blacks. As a result of the land grant college movement and the work of certain religious groups and the Freedmen's Bureau, a number of new institutions were established, especially in the South, for the benefit of freed slaves.

These postwar colleges for the most part fell into two categories of orientation. Although most of the colleges made noble efforts to provide a thorough liberal arts education for their students, the growth and development of the institutions were made possible by the fact that they tended to be technical schools, most of them hardly comparable to the best academic high schools of the period. Preparing black students for successful vocations was of necessity a chief concern, and this focus was encouraged also by the prevalent attitude in education that the emphasis should be on professional and technical preparation, that a liberal arts education was virtually useless amid the realities of everyday life.

A second influence on the nature of these institutions was the fact that many of them were founded by religious groups, and more had largely religious administrations and leadership — often white, and usually missionary-oriented. There were few colleges dominated by a black, intellectually oriented faculty and administration. The nature of these colleges remained largely the same throughout the late nineteenth and early twentieth centuries as more such institutions came into existence, many in the South and a few in such northern states as Ohio and Pennsylvania.

The situation began to change during the 1930s and 1940s with a rising interest in civil rights. During this time, black teachers in the public schools tended to accumulate more higher education credits than white teachers, in order to make up for the salary differentials that were imposed by race. The result was a relatively large pool of blacks with postbaccalaureate training. Some of these blacks began to be attracted to the black colleges, and their presence, combined with the new concern for civil rights, created a different atmosphere on the campuses of these institutions.

A major development occurred during 1947 and 1948 with the establishment of the National Scholarship Service and Fund for Negro Students. Through this organization, some of the more prestigious white institutions joined in the search for talented black students who could be encouraged and assisted in the process of being admitted to better or higher status institutions. Other black students found themselves doing postgraduate work in predominantly white universities as a result of the effort on the part of southern public institutions to avoid the most blatant violations of civil rights and still manage to exclude blacks from their universities; their solution was to grant tuition allowances to black students to take out of the state to other institutions where they were more welcome.

As increasing pressure was brought to bear on segregated state institutions, the response was an upgrading of black state colleges, with the creation of pseudo graduate and professional schools. However, by 1950 the Supreme Court had ruled that the segregation of black students in publicly supported graduate schools was illegal, and following the 1954 public school desegregation decision, state institutions were legally on their way to being open to all regardless of race, although this principle has certainly not been implemented without opposition and violence.

The launching of the first Soviet space satellite, Sputnik I, in 1957, brought on a wave of concern for improving the national education system. The National Defense Education Act focused resources and interest on the discovery of talent, and added governmental concern to that already being manifested by certain private institutions. Many more universities now began to view minority group, and especially black, communities as fruitful fields for recruiting academically promising students, and the number of black students in white institutions began to climb. As a result of this new interest, many of the traditionally black colleges were cut off from their supplies of top students. In addition, many institutions began to work toward the development of compensatory programs for their new populations of disadvantaged students. However, these colleges found themselves operating in a new area with no effective source of prior experience upon which to draw. Although the traditionally black institutions had had these kinds of concerns for years, they had been able to develop no special solutions; most had made curriculum adjustments, slowing the pace or lowering the quality of required achievement, and providing some remedial courses in the freshman year. For the most part, however, the quality of the efforts served to lend credence to the controversial criticisms of these institutions by Jencks and Reissman in the *Harvard Educational Review*. There were some exceptions to this general situation, such as Morgan State College, in Baltimore, which concentrated on the development of test-taking sophistication, and Dillard University, in New Orleans, which gave attention to remedial education, reading, and language enrichment. Institutions such as Howard, Fisk, Spellman, Morehouse, and Talladega prided themselves on attracting top black students and faculty members, and maintaining standards comparable to the other better institutions in the country.

However, whatever their accomplishments may have been in this area, there is little evidence that the black institutions were even consulted by the white colleges to investigate what they might have to offer. Most of the white institutions seem to have repeated the mistakes made by the black colleges earlier, especially in their assumption that traditional approaches to remedial education can provide an adequate compensatory effort. Nevertheless, the years from the late 1950s up to 1970 have been marked by increasing amounts of the same kind of effort, and a rapid expansion of the movement to include more minority group and disadvantaged students in the higher education population. The drive seems to have peaked during the 1968–69 school year, when almost half of the nation's colleges and universities were making some effort to recruit and/or to provide special services for students from disadvantaged backgrounds.

Most of these colleges were using various combinations of several basic practices, some of which are designed primarily to help disadvantaged students enter college, with others used to help them succeed once they had been admitted. Many institutions have their own recruiting programs, and offer substantial financial assistance for tuition and living expenses. Some offer special courses and programs prior to the freshman year to prepare students for admission. Counseling and tutoring services are made available with personal counseling concentrating on facilitating the adjustment of the student to a new environment, and academic counseling aimed at improving school skills and attitudes. Many colleges have tried special remedial courses, and have offered a variety of programs to improve study skills. In some institutions special curriculum programs have been offered, and some programs provide for an extended period of time to complete degree requirements.

The rapid growth of the movement to open higher education to greater varieties of young people ran into a number of obstacles, however, which have shown themselves during the 1969–70 school year. One such problem is the very growth of the effort itself; as the number of these new students on the campuses has increased, college personnel have begun to realize that the success of educating them does not depend simply on good intentions; the complexities of the problem are being manifested in new forms every day. Many of the programs have been largely political responses to recently increased pressures from blacks and other minority groups for inclusion in all phases of the mainstream of life in the society. At this period, however, other pressures are competing insistently with the moral claims of disadvantaged groups. Money available for such innovative programs has decreased, or at least seems to be frozen at past levels; preoccupation with the war and the exploitation of the environment has occupied a good deal of the moral energy of those who might be expected to be concerned with the problem. It should be noted that some of those states which must remain particularly sensitive to the moods of their comparatively large minority populations have continued to make some progress in this direction; New York, for example, has been the scene of a good deal of effort toward devising an effective open enrollment policy for public institutions. However, the effort is tainted by the haste of political expediency, and its educational effectiveness is gravely in doubt. Even while similar political responses continue to be in evidence where they appear to be absolutely necessary, the frustrating effect of current economic priorities cannot be overestimated. Financial support for new and even many old programs and policies is simply drying up. Even if we succeed in recruiting the students and know what to do for them once they are in the colleges, if we cannot give them adequate financial support, our efforts will not stand a chance of success. And the cost of a successful effort, as we are beginning to see, will not be modest.

This brief background summary of efforts in the field to date is not intended to be encouraging. It can be seen that the more privileged, white institutions have not yet begun to contribute all that they may be expected to provide for the improvement of higher educational opportunity. One thing that should be emphasized is the fact that traditionally black institutions have made the major effort at compensatory education for minority groups over these past 100 years. Only very recently have white universities and community colleges undertaken a share in the task, and even now, statistics on the distribution of students show that the older, black institutions still serve approximately 65 percent of black college students in four-year programs, and 45 to 50 percent if the figures for two-year community college student populations are taken into account. There does appear to be some slight shift on the part of the white institutions from the mere discovery of talent toward the task of compensating for social and educational disadvantages, the *development* of talent. There seems to be a movement away from the traditional dependence on testing to greater emphasis on personal characteristics and previous pattern of social coping; from remedial education to heavier use of small-group and individual tutorials; from concern with the dispersal of students throughout the campus for the sake of integration to greater attention to minority student concern for group identification, interaction, and solidarity. There have even been some efforts toward a greater reflection of the background and ethnic identity of these new students in the curriculum and the administration of these institutions.

I say my summary is not intended to be encouraging; at this point I should be identifying those practices that have been particularly successful. Without intending to demean the considerable effort put into the many programs in the field, I am nevertheless forced to conclude that there are no generic patterns or practices that fit this description. I must note that some part of the problem may be the lack of effective evaluation efforts in the field; the closest thing to an important research work in the area has been the Clark and Plotkin follow-up of students aided by the National Scholarship Service and Fund for Negro Students, which revealed that most of the students included did successfully complete their college programs; the report made no effort to evaluate any of the educational programs or practices involved. I base most of my observations on the work of a team with which I have been involved, which has made a one-year study of programs in the area. From the results of this work it is possible to gain some impressions of the complex problems involved and even some hunches concerning the direction we should take in the future.

No aspect of the effort to include disadvantaged students in higher education has been without serious problems starting from the processes of recruitment and admission. In an extension of the earlier concern with talent search practices, many institutions that have not yet served larger numbers of minority group students are simply adding those communities that do have large populations of minority group people to their recruitment circuit. Others use alumni to identify and encourage minority group students to apply. The use of the National Scholarship Service and Fund for Negro Students as a black student finding service has not been reduced in volume, but has decreased in proportion. There is a growing competition among institutions for able minority students; potential recruits are wined and dined, as well as offered competitive scholarships, in a process of seduction comparable to the earlier efforts to grab off top athletes. The less prestigious or public institutions have been less concerned with traditional indices of potential and more concerned with having a large enough population of minority students to avoid accusations of racism and discrimination. All these efforts have reduced the number and quality of students available to attend those institutions that have traditionally served minority group students.

Once past the confusion of efforts and methods for obtaining a pool of disadvantaged students for the various institutions willing to accept them, one would expect that we would have a process by which the transition from high school to college could be facilitated. If an institution is determined to serve large numbers of disadvantaged and minority group young people, it must realize the futility of depending on standard testing procedures. But no institution seems to have viable alternative criteria to guide the admissions process. Most institutions claim to be concerned with the personal characteristics of students, yet our best device for ascertaining these characteristics is the personal interview and the comments of people who have known the student. With an insufficient analysis of our experience in using these criteria, we have no basis for making predictions in which we can place confidence. An alternative at the opposite extreme to selection on the basis of test scores is open admission in its many variations, a method which solves the problem by avoiding it but immediately confronts us with a variety of new problems related to placement and treatment, not to mention resources and facilities, problems for which I see no reasonable solutions at hand or even on the horizon. Maybe the best that we can say is that institutions are at various stages of making up their minds about what kind of students they want and admitting them accordingly, and that there is as yet no really firm process for doing so. Most institutions seem to be superficially committed to developing heterogeneous populations as long as they are homogeneous enough to enable the institution to continue operating without significant change. Even in these institutions and systems which either have had or are moving toward open enrollment the innovation is deceptive, because even if a youngster is assured entrance into the system, he is not assured a higher education experience as it is traditionally conceived, although he may have a slightly enhanced opportunity to qualify for formal participation in this type of education. On the whole, however, we must conclude that the administrative processes of open admission, like those still prevalent in almost all higher education institutions, are still more influenced by considerations of meritocracy than those of democracy.

Since the development of academic competence is one of the common goals implicit to these efforts, one would expect that the greatest amount of activity and emphasis would be placed on changes in the collegiate curriculum that are designed to insure the success of this development for the new student population. However, it is in this area of curriculum development that it is most difficult to perceive meaningful innovation.

The developments in this area are anemic in relation to the magnitude of the problem. The most controversial and prominent change is in the area of ethnic studies, where many forces have resulted in a plethora of activities designed to append black, Puerto Rican, or chicano studies to the existing curriculum. Many of these have been hastily conceived and implemented and are likely to be a source of embarrassment to minority group students as well as to the institutions. A few institutions have responded with a general review of their curriculum content and practices with a view to revision and general improvement of the processes. These developments, of which the *Thirteen College Project* is an example, have not been specific to the characteristics of needs of the minority group population but have focused on improved teaching in general. Where large numbers of students are involved, varieties of preparatory curriculum forms have been developed whereby this new population of students is held at bay or given special treatment until they qualify for admission to the regular program. Most institutions are moving away from earlier emphases on formal remedial courses toward the use of tutorials and independent study in attacks on specific problems. Probably the most subtle new emphasis is in the development of new degree programs which either reflect the special interests of many of these new students or represent somewhat less respectable routes to the academic credential. All of these developments, honestly or dishonestly conceived, have made some changes in the academic opportunity structure for disadvantaged students. They have not, however, appreciably changed the quality of the university's service to this population.

The problem which recurs in any discussion of the effort to provide higher education for significant numbers of disadvantaged students is the question of financial aid. The questions and pitfalls here may comprise the core problem in the area: in order to make an appreciable increase in the amount of minority group students, we will have to see that they are sufficiently subsidized.

Earlier, scholarships, in the form of tuition grants and living stipends, were available, although not always adequate. In addition, there was the problem of the method of distribution of these funds to those to whom they were granted; many minority group students came to feel that the scholarship was little more than a new form of welfare, as a result of the demeaning way in which the money was doled out to them, with no effort to conceal the suspicion on the part of the institution that these particular students probably lacked the discretion to handle the money wisely. As the programs continue and expand, we not only have the problem of maintaining and distributing the existing level of support for individual students, but also the problem of increasing support, since in most instances it is viewed by students as insufficient. We must add to this the problem of a limited or even a shrinking reservoir of money. Many of these programs were initially able to attract support from external sources such as foundations because they were regarded as particularly innovative; as they become institutionalized, they must depend more heavily on the funds of the college. The utilization of institutional or public funds to support special programs is viewed negatively by some segments of the population who see funds and resources used for this purpose as being competitive with or reductive of resources available for the traditional populations served by these institutions. I see no really novel solution to this problem as perceived by those majority group members who have recently joined the upwardly mobile population. Some people are suggesting the wide use of cooperative work-study programs, in which all students, and particularly economically disadvantaged ones, extend their period of study and divide each school year between alternate sessions of study and remunerative work. This model, most highly developed at Northeastern University in Boston, shows promise so long as jobs can be found that pay well enough to enable students to save sufficient funds to cover the alternate periods of study.

However, we must realize that even in those instances where the cost of higher education for the individual is modest, or is completely covered by financial assistance, the student must also consider the income loss to his economically deprived family as he is kept out of the labor market by his extended period of education. So long as the cost of higher education is viewed as a personal or private cost to be borne by the beneficiary, and is not regarded as an investment by the society in the development of human potential, this problem will remain unsolved. Higher education as a societal investment must not only be free but must carry with it subsidies to meet the other responsibilities a potential student feels are his.

In addition to the problem of individual student support, however, there is the question of support for the special programs that may be involved. Here, it is important to realize that what is needed is not simply the bare minimum necessary to operate the program, but the amount necessary to give it parity of social status with other sections and departments of the university.

One of the most significant developments associated with the effort to democratize access to higher education has occurred most often without institutional sponsorship. For a long time many of us have suspected that there are noncognitive factors that are significantly associated with achievement in any sphere and particularly in higher education. Increasingly, it appears that those students who find in their college experiences islands of cultural, ethnic, or political identity and strength, also find the college experience more acceptable and tend to show patterns of lower attrition. The emergence of the black cultural center, of patterns of residential assignment that maintain cultural solidarity in living arrangements, and of political and social action-oriented ethnic organizations are neither accidental nor incidental developments on the college scene. Even where they may have been political in origin they are perceived by many to serve a major pedagogical function. We have not been sufficiently sensitive to the social-psychological burden carried by the isolated minority group student who is constantly called upon to be the example, the representative, the interpreter of his culture, and the "house nigger" for his institution. We have given insufficient attention to the possible deleterious effects such pressures have on the total development of these young people. Our concern for integration has overridden a concern for the optimal development of the individual student, especially those from minority backgrounds. Fortunately, many institutions have responded positively to the message and have given support to this development. Others, frightened at the prospect of "black power" or similar bugaboos, have discouraged and resisted this development, probably unaware that their resistance served to strengthen such movements as well as to defeat the purposes of the special program.

It is not easy for an institution to react wisely to movements toward cultural nationalism. There are many pitfalls. While students from minority groups need to be able to identify with others of similar cultural background, at the same time there is need for them to be able to mingle with a variety of other students, and to act within the larger group freely and significantly. The institution must do its part to maintain this delicate balance of social interaction; it must not respond to the demand for an opportunity for separatism with a system of enforced segregation. The problem is compounded by the fact that, the greater and more voluble the demand for cultural nationalism, the harder it is to maintain the balance in the face of the majority group reaction to these efforts at independence. A somewhat simpler and more easily soluble problem is the availability of physical facilities for these efforts. The important need here is for the institution to be willing to provide facilities of obvious quality, comparable to those provided for other types of activities, and in locations that clearly indicate that the group is as much a part of the university as any other. It may seem superfluous to make this point, but in too many schools, the hasty response to minority student pressure has been the provision of shabby facilities, as isolated as possible from the mainstream of student life. Such "other side of the tracks" treatment can only serve to further isolate and alienate the students it is so important to include.

The presence of a significant proportion of minority group adults in the teaching and administrative staffs of the university will also serve as a means of making the new kind of student feel more a part of the institution. As long as he can perceive only his difference from the staff and main student body of the college, the disadvantaged student will perceive it as an alien institution, and himself as part of an alien group, whose presence is merely tolerated. The presence of adults of his ethnic background will contribute to the student's sense that the college is his school, too, and that he has a stake in it. It should quickly be added that the efforts of these institutions to increase minority representation by quickly staffing ethnic studies programs or community centers with such personnel is not adequate to the need. Part of the problem is that these programs are already perceived as tangential. We need to have minority group faces in the chemistry laboratory, the history classroom, the psychology center. There must be a minority group presence of sufficient size and status to be regarded as a part of the main event and not as an exotic sideshow.

A great many of these problems derive from the origin of the programs we are discussing. Too often they have been spawned out of crisis situations, such as a political response to minority group pressures or as ways to fulfill the stipulations of special grants. Some institutions have begun such programs out of a desire to be up-to-date with what is currently fashionable in education; others undoubtedly have more genuine humanitarian concerns, for it must be conceded that the intellectual community has at least long had a tradition of liberal thought. No matter what the motivation, however, the majority of these programs have been poorly conceived and too hastily thrown together. Perhaps we should note as exceptions those institutions that began with the recruitment of a very few exceptionally talented minority group students and who persist in this limited practice, perhaps regarding it as the most they can do to fulfill any social responsibility they may have. These colleges are at least to be commended for caution, though their caution seems to overshadow concern for the real problem, since little in their efforts speaks specifically to the complex questions emerging in this field. Perhaps the best policy for those institutions that do feel a responsibility in the area is to conduct a searching examination of the real extent of their commitment, the kind of students they wish to serve, and the extent of their resources before proceeding to plan a program accordingly.

Once the institution has at least committed itself to the extent of establishing a special program, there are often problems of control and administration. Because the area is regarded as more political than other areas of academic concern, special project administrators and faculty may be deprived of the independence they need to work out a really effective program. The needs of these special students are too often subjugated to the political and public-relations needs of the institution as a whole.

The importance of a careful definition of the students to be served relates also to the kind of program and curriculum to be planned. A group of "disadvantaged" students may not necessarily be homogeneous simply by fact of disadvantagement. There may be many variations in the population from which students are to be drawn. Corresponding variations in the program may be needed to suit the special needs of students with different characteristics.

These areas of weakness certainly constitute a rather pessimistic picture, and this discouraging situation may be related to the essential nature of the problem at hand. For many years, higher education has served three functions: human intellectual development, professional skills development, and credentialing. In our concern for the democratization of access to higher education, the three have been greatly confused. Most of the concern for democratization has been with the credentialing function. But in response to the new pressures, many institutions have insisted that their major function is *not* credentialing, but professional skills and intellectual development, and that the credential cannot be separate from this.

An honest look at the history of higher education should reveal to all but the most biased that we have found ways in the past to admit and provide the collegiate credential to selected members of the population whose "qualifications" — or lack of them — have been not unlike those of the new populations we are considering, except that these former students have had some additional characteristic such as money, higher social status, strong political contacts, or athletic ability. Because of the efforts of the institutions involved, these kinds of students have received the baccalaureate degree, a necessary credential for admission to many of the more prestigious places in the societal mainstream. Many of these special cases function quite adequately, since, as Ivar Berg has pointed out, there is not necessarily a high positive relationship between the credential required for a particular career and the tasks that must be performed in that career.

Clearly, then, if we could separate out the credentialing function and universalize the opportunity for that, the problem would be simplified numerically. But we would still be faced with the problem of building intellectual and professional skills on an inadequate educational base. It is futile for the university to tackle this problem divorced from its roots in elementary and secondary education. Yet since the university *is* being called upon to provide high-level intellectual development for those students who are demanding more than a credential and who come with poor previous preparation, this very valid observation nonetheless does not relieve the university of responsibility for seeking a pedagogical solution. The educational habilitation of young adults with academically dysfunctional learning patterns is really the core of the problem. We have not yet reached that stage of pedagogical sophistication where the analysis of learning behaviors can lead to the design of formal learning experiences and the development of appropriate learning environments. These are the central aspects of the task at hand. The problem is not just a technical one. Another crucial consideration is the availability of human social interactions and opportunities for political expression that serve to motivate rather than frustrate. Solutions offered at this time do not address these aspects of the problem and will in all likelihood continue to fail for this reason. A possible reason for the failure to develop such solutions is that the problem has not been conceptualized in these ways. When these kinds of problems are brought together with the political economy of the disadvantaged individual's access to higher education, all but the most foolishly optimistic must realize that our *current* efforts are doomed to failure.

From these observations, it is possible to derive some general ideas concerning new directions for our efforts. It is clear that the question of financial resource support for students and programs is one of the most critical problems. If we do not have massive funds available for higher education and the tangential costs of income substitution for the families involved, we simply cannot talk seriously about higher education for large numbers of low-income young people. Even at the present level of commitment, many institutions are finding the effort too costly, because of the necessary special services and facilities. The current trend toward loans, while better than nothing, still does not provide an adequate answer. Many of the young people in the target populations still have to be sold on the idea of seeking a college education in the first place; they certainly can't be expected to be willing to go deeply into debt to obtain one. Given the current conservative political trend, probably the best strategy to follow is to seek broad state and federal support of institutions of higher education and students in general, without particular attention to financial need and ethnic background. If access to the institutions becomes easier for all, it will be easier for poor youngsters. When funds are available for individual assistance, they should be distributed as money to which the students are entitled, not as a dole; young people engaged in the effort to develop their talents more fully are contributing members of the labor force. Perhaps a monthly allowance would prove the best method of distribution, and the amount available should take into account obligations of family support.

A pragmatic strategy for the present political situation may be to appeal to the professed patriotism of the conservative majority by seeking expanded veterans' benefits; since minority group youth are particularly susceptible to the military draft, this move would tend to increase the higher education opportunity for one segment of the population.

All of these strategies are based on the obvious conclusion that fiscal problems currently operate to drastically limit efforts in the area and without their solution, other problems will not be soluble. However, although the financial problem is not to be solved without support at the highest levels, political realities and the moral responsibilities of higher education are such that ways must be found within the limits of current and modestly expanded budgets to begin rapid movement in this direction.

Unquestionably a problem of huge proportions is the amount of expanded facilities that will be required if we are to serve great numbers of new students who might not have been able to afford a postsecondary education previously. One solution may be to utilize community colleges to serve all students entering higher education and to transform all four-year colleges into senior colleges serving those students in their third and fourth years of posthigh school study. In a sense, this proposal amounts to little more than a postponement of the problem, since it means simply extending the public secondary school education by two years and postponing the selection process; but by doing so, we could at least relieve senior colleges of the obligation to provide the first two years of this education, freeing some resources and facilities, and allowing students an additional two years to make a decision concerning higher education. In the meantime, we would hope that more resources would be available for the building of more college facilities.

This suggestion is perhaps a too utopian solution in the sense that it certainly cannot be put into effect tomorrow. A more immediate approach should perhaps be simply to aim for a more equal distribution of talent and resources. If institutions are really determined to attack this problem, perhaps they should ask seriously why those colleges which supposedly offer the best education and reputedly have the best teaching talent should continue to serve only the supposedly best students. A better distribution of teaching talent and student quality would go far to equalize educational opportunity.

In addition, a work-study plan of operation can increase the number of students served immediately by any one institution in the sense that more students can be admitted to present facilities in any one year. This procedure could serve as a method of buying time for expansion as well as a method for providing support for indigent students.

The problem of college admissions procedures also suggests both long-term and short-term efforts at solution. These institutions are still interested in serving the intellectual development function, and justifiably so; but we must also face the problem of democratizing the credentialing function. A decision that could be made within the individual institution is to devote half of its resources to the function of credentialing, with this half of its student body selected at random from an actively recruited, representative pool of high school graduates, and to concentrate intellectual development activities more particularly on the second half of the student body, selected after offering to potential applicants greater specificity as to the kind of students wanted; within this second group, a wider variety of characteristics might be sought, including membership in a minority group and more varied patterns of intellectual function.

This possible solution for individual colleges demonstrates that it is not necessary to move completely away from meritocratic considerations; it is possible to move both ways at once. If we were able to develop broader criteria for estimating excellence of potential, it might be possible to devise some sort of scheme whereby promising high school graduates could be assured admission to one of their top three choices of college to the extent that no more than 50 percent of available places are filled; after this point, the remaining 50 percent would be available to other students on a lottery basis, with some effort meanwhile being made to arrive at a method by which all students could enjoy some element of choice in their college assignment and be assured a high degree of quality in their educational treatment.

The rationale for this sort of compromise is the fact that there *is* a place in higher education for attention to the development of an intellectual elite, though the term may be distasteful to us; democratic values do not preclude the optimal development of available resources, and though this may not be an infallible plan for doing so, at least it provides that 50 percent of our educational facilities are devoted to the more democratic goal of credentialing for larger numbers of young people, while the other half of the facilities are used for the development of professional skills and intellectual excellence.

The problem of admissions cannot be divorced from the problem of educational planning and treatment. The principle of symmetry as advanced by James Coleman, a member of the Commission on Tests, in a brief to the College Entrance Examination Board provides an appropriate conceptual frame for discussing the problem. Coleman argues that students, as well as universities, should have the benefit of rich information about each other in the mating process; the student should have as much information about the institution as the institution has about him. An extension of this principle involves the appropriate matching of the characteristics and needs of the student with the characteristics and resources of the institution. In order to serve both aspects of the principle of symmetry, data-gathering procedures associated with the admissions process must be revised. We need to have available for students making choices about institutions, as well as for administrators making choices about students, detailed information concerning commitments, strengths, weaknesses, and resources — information more detailed than that provided by commercial college guides or the typical college catalog. Even more important is the need for detailed and qualitative information descriptive of the intellectual and personal-social functioning of students — their strengths, weaknesses, and specific patterns of need to be met if their development is to be optimized.

In the area of curriculum design, there are at least three concerns that should be important influences in the drive to serve broader populations: (1) the utilization and modification of mental postures and learning patterns in inefficient or less well-prepared young adult learners; (2) a problem faced in work with all students, the development of professional competence and expansion of intellectual development; and (3) the problem of sufficiently involving the student in the developmental task, the process of somehow bridging the gap between the student's perception of the institution as irrelevant to the concerns of his life so far, and the institution's own, sometimes overblown, notion of its own relevance for life as it is institutionally conceived.

Our earlier expressed concern with detailed, sophisticated qualitative information on the nature of the learning process in young adults who have not traditionally functioned well in academic settings could provide the data from which appropriate teaching-learning strategies can be developed. These strategies may range from shifts in the context and nature of the material to be mastered through the devising of alternate input systems for the acquisition of knowledge banks for those students who suffer from major deficits in information as well as impaired skills for acquiring it, to the design of elaborate instructional procedures that utilize sophisticated devices to monitor learner behavior in response to materials that are programed to complement idiosyncratic patterns of affective-cognitive function.

To supplement activity at any one of these levels we will need to continue and expand what appears to be the relatively successful use of tutorials and individual work with students around their specific learning needs. Independent study centers have the advantage of not negatively identifying a student "in trouble" since they are also used for bright students who wish to supplement their regular school experience as well as for students working at a slower pace who require some kind of assistance.

As is the case in elementary and secondary schools, our focus on special populations calls attention to general inefficiencies in pedagogical practice for all students; higher education's responsibility for intellectual development requires constant work at improving curriculum. In this area, the Thirteen College Curriculum Program, directed specifically at the populations served by 13 predominantly black institutions, provides a useful model insofar as resources and time are set aside to allow college teachers to think about and work on improvement of collegiate instruction. Attention to curriculum development at the college level is long overdue, and is critical for disadvantaged students in particular, as well as being entirely appropriate to higher education in general.

I find it difficult to abandon my preoccupation with the development of strategies for directly attacking the problem of improvement of cognitive function, but I cannot be oblivious to the mounting evidence that fundamental changes in the character of cognitive function may not be susceptible to direct attack, although derivative changes may flow from work in the affective area, which Zigler argues is more malleable than the cognitive. Hence, the third aspect of effort at improvement in curriculum development is in this area we call motivation and task involvement. Here the problem is to make the relevance of the essential aspects of the learning tasks of higher education more apparent to the youngsters served. Information management, mastery of knowledge, and intellectual competence and skills are not irrelevant to real life in the society, but the society has moved to distort and prostitute the purposes toward which these knowledges, skills, and competencies are utilized. When the university becomes an accomplice in this process of distortion, we are subverting the goals and objectives that are fundamental to our purposes. When science is used to exploit and victimize humanity instead of to help it, it is indeed hard to perceive the relevance of the sciences. When economics is used to exploit, colonize, and enslave, it becomes difficult to excite an honest student about the study of this discipline. When I as a professor use my discipline to achieve my own personal ends and glory rather than to further more general social goals, my students cannot be expected to respect me or use me as a model. Many young people see in the university a haven for the glorification of knowledge for knowledge's sake, rather than a concern for knowledge for the service of humanity; a mecca for the individual academic entrepreneur rather than a community for scholars devoted to the facilitation of human development; an appendage to the military-industrial complex committed to the continued subjugation of third-world people. Such perceptions make difficult, if not impossible, their identification with these institutions.

When the university's resources for intellectual and professional development are made unacceptable to students because of the institution's complicity with reactionary political or economic forces, the educational relevance of conflicting views of the college becomes obvious. We may win the battle of democratized access to higher education only to find that those for whom the struggle was waged want no part of these institutions to which we have opened the doors. As important as are the problems of access, of even greater importance are the problems of access to what. It is increasingly clear that the university must not only protect the opportunity of students to express themselves through social and political action, it must also become identified with the struggle to understand and guide the social and political development of the society. The absence of either can interfere not only with the politico-social development of our students, indeed it can — by reducing or preventing their involvement in the processes of higher education — preclude their further intellectual development through the university. If the problems of the outside world make students unable to perceive the relevance of the academic disciplines, then the school must turn its attention to the outside world in order to relate these disciplines to the problems of that world and *make* itself more relevant; for we must realize that if our students perceive us as irrelevant, then we *are* irrelevant to their purposes; if we cannot foster and hand down our knowledge because students have no respect for us, then we have no useful function to serve for them. In this extremely critical time of social conflict and political resistance, we must see, as many of our students feel, that the university is one of the few hopes we have for fostering change; if the universities, havens of freedom and thought, choose to do nothing, they will be unattractive to increasingly large numbers of students. For many of those who continue to turn to the university and those of us faculty members who remain cloistered and insulated from the realities of a society desperately in need of intellectual and moral leadership there is likely to be little that is alive, creative, and productive. It is well to remember that, during the Nazi domination of Europe, many of the university faculties that were dominated by collaborators and the complacent became stultified and sterile; it was among those scholars who chose not to acquiesce, but instead to go underground, to resist and to help turn back the tide of social and political disaster, that creative scholarship, and true relevance, flourished. The United States of America may not yet be on the way to fascism, despite the evidence that so many of our young people, and I, could easily cite, but they and our society need that the university move more actively to democratize access to its resources as well as to utilize its resources in the active defense and advancement of the democratic society.

References

Berg, Ivar, "Rich Man's Qualifications for Poor Man's Jobs: Are Employers Demanding Too Much Education for the Jobs They Offer?" *Trans-action,* Vol. VI, March 1969, pp. 45–50.

Clark, Kenneth B., and Plotkin, Lawrence, *The Negro Student at Integrated Colleges.* New York: National Scholarship Service and Fund for Negro Students, 1963.

Coleman, James S., "The Principle of Symmetry in College Choice," pp. 19–32 in Commission on Tests, *Report of the Commission on Tests: II. Briefs*. New York: College Entrance Examination Board, 1970, 194 pp.

Institute for Services to Education. *Journey into Discovery: The Thirteen College Curriculum Program.* Washington, D.C.: Institute for Services to Education, 1969.

Jencks, Christopher, and Riesman, David, "The American Negro College." *Harvard Educational Review,* No. 37, Winter, 1967.

Zigler, E., "Rigidity and Social Reinforcement Effects in the Performance of Institutionalized and Noninstitutionalized Normal and Retarded Children." *Journal of Personality,* No. 31, 1963, pp. 258–269.

Response to Edmund W. Gordon's Paper

By Helen S. Astin

As a respondent to Dr. Gordon's paper, I shall attempt to reemphasize some of the important comments made by him in his paper as well as respond, in part, to some findings reported by other colleagues during this conference. I would also like to share with you some of our findings and knowledge gained thus far from our national study of special programs for disadvantaged youth.

There is no question that the lack of adequate funding and the decrease in available money for special and innovative programs in education is a major hindrance and concern to all those involved in the education of disadvantaged youth. However, our slow pace in true innovation, our repetitiveness of efforts, and the lack of evaluation of how effective our teaching methods and programs are presents a crucial and bothersome obstacle to the educational movement for equal educational opportunity in higher education. Moreover, one is truly pressed hard to find innovations in curricular and in pedagogical approaches.

Two other points made by Dr. Gordon need reemphasis. He has raised the question of whether we have examined how youngsters manage to adjust to their new and often lonely college environments, and whether we have tried to make the transition and adjustment easier and less painful. In the past, we have been concerned with the adjustment of foreign students to American campus life. We have encouraged the development of international clubs and organizations on campus; we have even allocated dormitories or other campus facilities for international students. We have done so in full knowledge and acceptance of the fact that these foreign students need the experience of a cultural solidarity and the security that the company of other foreign students can provide. There is a parallel here. I, for one, was at first upset at the demands of black students for separate facilities, but I have become much more emphatic with their need to be together and separate, to share their past experiences, and then emerge into the new environment at their own pace and style.

Another point I would like to bring up is that our experiences thus far suggest the value of tutorials over remedial courses. Very often remedial courses are repetitive, whereas tutorials allow greater freedom and respect for individual needs and differences. This fact has been recognized and the trend today is more toward tutorial aid instead of remedial courses. In our study, 11 of the 19 case study institutions offer tutorials compared to only 6 institutions that still emphasize remedial courses.

In a study by the University Research Corporation, we have also noted that the reported retention rate among disadvantaged students in special programs is higher than the one observed with college students in general. Moreover, the students we have interviewed express a great deal of positive feelings toward the special program and the experience in college in general. Also, the attitudes expressed by the university staff and faculty were very positive. A comment often made by the faculty was that having a special program for under-prepared students on the campus provides a continuous challenge to them; ". . . we have started to question our teaching methods, and the total educational process . . . ."

Although the problems and obstacles are numerous, there are still many procedures that could be changed and remedied. For example, a very bothersome problem, in my opinion, is the large turnover of key personnel in these programs. Their experience with these programs, although sometimes very short, makes them very desirable to larger and richer institutions when these colleges decide to become involved in the education of minority students. These institutions offer more in status as well as in money, and thus are successful in recruiting those with experience in special programs. However, this upper mobility, which is good for the individual, often hurts the program and ultimately the students in the program. During our own study, the turnover I speak of became one of the difficulties in our data collection. The letter of invitation for participation in the study would reach the program director, and by the time we would call to schedule an appointment with him, we would find out that he had accepted a new position and that we should get in touch with the new director or the acting director.

A number of institutions provide courses of a remedial nature without awarding credit to the students who complete the course. This is completely contradictory to our knowledge of rewards as an essential component in the learning process. Although we are fully aware of it, we still have not been able to improvise so we can manage the total system of degree credits and their differential allocation on the basis of individual differences with respect to the learning pace and style. Apropos to this, I would like to say that our own data supports the notion of a five-year baccalaureate program for students who can manage best with a reduced load, suggesting a greater flexibility for credit earning.

I would also like to suggest that each program director and his staff assume greater responsibility in public relations work with the total institution. We have interviewed faculty members and students at institutions that house active programs who did not know of their institution's interest and effort in programs for educationally disadvantaged students. Not only would I like to see the whole academic community fully informed and involved, but I would like to propose a greater exchange and shifting of students and faculties. I would like to see some of the chaired professors, for example, become truly involved in the education of underprepared students. I would even like to propose some changes in our present reward system. For example, an outstanding professor would be asked to teach a class of high risk students. And as a reward for his success in the development of these students, he might be offered a six-month sabbatical. We reward the publishing of books and other publications — why not reward cognitive growth in students effected by a teacher or by his innovative curriculum and teaching methods.

Before I close, I would like to emphasize again how little we know about what truly makes a difference as far as educational progress and growth is concerned. There is no question that the need for rigorous and evaluative research on what kinds of students benefit from what kinds of experiences is of paramount importance and urgency.

Lack of Money:
A Barrier to Higher Education

By Humphrey Doermann

Even though the amount of money available to college students has increased dramatically in the last 10 years, and even though an increasing percentage of our high school graduates — from all races and all income levels — now goes on to college, it still remains true that lack of sufficient financial support remains one of the major barriers to higher education in the United States. Students who could and should benefit from education after high school are diverted from doing so because they lack the money. Others who do go on must incur unduly large debts and invest too many hours in student jobs. For them, both the freedom to choose which kind of college they attend, and the quality and continuity of their training suffer accordingly. It is often difficult to demonstrate these truths convincingly to the private groups and to the legislatures which might be able to provide more money than they already have, or to generations, now past college age, that went to school at a time when formal education after high school was regarded as the privilege of the few, rather than the right of anyone who might benefit from it and wanted it. But those who have worked closely with any broad sampling of high school and college students know that the financial barriers are real, and that reducing their size and impact deserves our most urgent attention.

This need seems sufficiently clear so that, for the present at least, it seems unnecessary to argue the point further in general terms. Instead, this paper undertakes two specific and related tasks: It offers one possible framework for appraising which kinds of students participate least in higher education, and how much money they may need if that participation rate is to increase significantly. And it suggests some of the issues related to the provision of increased financial aid, issues which clearly need further discussion if this aid is to be effective in broadening educational opportunity.

Joint Distribution Tables:
United States Male High School Graduates

In Tables 1-4, I have estimated how the current year's crop of 1,450,000 male high school graduates and the roughly 148,000 black male high school graduates would be classified jointly by verbal scholastic aptitude, and by the pretax income of their families. Each of the two populations (the 1,450,000 and the 148,000) are presented in two ways: first, in total, and second, classified by whether or not they are estimated to attend college within a year of high school graduation. In the left-hand column of each table, beneath each category of family income, the amount of money listed in parentheses is the amount the College Scholarship Service (CSS) estimated a three-child family in normal circumstances might be able to contribute toward a college education. The College Scholarship Service estimates of family contribution are those used in setting the original freshman stipends for today's college seniors. The CSS tables used for today's freshmen required smaller family contributions at the same income levels. If one wished to estimate the size of individual pools of *both* male and female high school graduates, one could multiply each of the individual cell figures in the table by a factor of two and arrive at an adequate working esti-

Table 1. Estimated Joint Distribution
of All United States Male High School Graduates, 1969-70:
Verbal Scholastic Aptitude and Family Income

Family Income (Possible Family Contribution to Son's College Costs)	Verbal Scholastic Aptitude Test Scores			
	200–299	300–449	450–800	Totals
Less than $4,600 (Less than $270)	116,000	113,000	25,000	254,000
$4,600 to $7,499 ($270 to $729)	102,000	139,000	44,000	285,000
$7,500 to $10,699 ($730 to $1,419)	89,000	143,000	60,000	292,000
$10,700 to $16,199 ($1,420 to $3,079)	78,000	146,000	82,000	306,000
$16,200 and over ($3,080 and over)	59,000	131,000	123,000	313,000
Totals	444,000	672,000	334,000	1,450,000

Source: Humphrey Doermann, *Crosscurrents in College Admissions,* New York: Teachers College Press, 1970, Table A-8.

Table 2. Estimated Joint Distribution of United States Black Male High School Graduates, 1969-70: Verbal Scholastic Aptitude and Family Income*

Family Income (Possible Family Contribution to Son's College Costs)	Verbal Scholastic Aptitude Test Scores			
	200-299	300-449	450-800	Totals
Less than $4,600 (Less than $270)	45,980	11,270	750	58,000
$4,600 to $7,499 ($270 to $729)	21,320	10,010	670	32,000
$7,500 to $10,699 ($730 to $1,419)	16,630	9,290	1,080	27,000
$10,700 to $16,199 ($1,420 to $3,079)	12,170	9,130	1,600	22,900
$16,200 and over ($3,080 and over)	3,200	3,800	1,100	8,100
Totals	99,300	43,500	5,200	148,000

* This table is derived from a similar distribution constructed for 1964–65 in Humphrey Doermann, *Crosscurrents in College Admissions*, pp. 48–49 and 159–162. The number of black male high school graduates was derived from an unpublished summary of black enrollees in grade 12 in high school, adjusted for probable percentage not graduating, and also adjusted for projected enrollment increase between 1968 and 1969. Family incomes were projected forward five years, at the same rate that nonwhite family incomes increased from 1962 to 1967, as reported in U.S. Bureau of the Census, *Income in 1967 of Families in the United States*, Series P-60, No. 59 (April 18, 1969), Washington, D.C.: U.S. Government Printing Office, p. 21.

mate. Thus, for example, one may read from Table 1 that approximately 254,000 male high school graduates (131,000 plus 123,000) are able to score 300 or above on the verbal sections of the College Board's Scholastic Aptitude Test (SAT), and *also* come from families earning $16,200 or more. (This estimate of 254,000, multiplied by two, equals 508,000, or the estimated number of male and female high school graduates.) These families, in turn, were estimated in 1966 by the CSS to be able to contribute, on the average, $3,080 or more toward a son's or daughter's college education. If the CSS guidelines used for setting 1969–70 stipends had been used in calculating Table 1, the family contribution figure would have been $1,980 instead of $3,080. I shall discuss this change in expected contribution later.

If one reads Table 2 with the same limiting conditions (verbal scholastic aptitude of 300 or better, family income of $16,200 or more) one estimates that

4,900 black male high school graduates met these conditions. Table 3 — again looking at the same two corresponding cells — estimates that of the 254,000 male high school graduates described this way, 244,000 will attend college within a year and 10,000 will not; Table 4 suggests that of the 4,900 black students enumerated, 4,230 are likely to attend college and 670 are not.

(The scoring range of the Scholastic Aptitude Test ranges from 200 (low) to 800 (high) with the median of those taking the test each year roughly 500.

**Table 3. Estimated Joint Distribution
of All United States Male High School Graduates, 1969-70:
Verbal Scholastic Aptitude and Family Income.***
**Top Figure in Each Cell Represents Estimated Number
of Students in College; Bottom (Parentheses) Figure
Represents Estimated Number Not in College**

Family Income (Possible Family Contribution to Son's College Costs)	Verbal Scholastic Aptitude Test Scores			
	200–299	300–449	450–800	Totals
Less than $4,600	25,000	34,000	16,000	75,000
(Less than $270)	(91,000)	(79,000)	(9,000)	(179,000)
$4,600 to $7,499	27,000	62,000	38,000	127,000
($270 to $729)	(75,000)	(77,000)	(6,000)	(158,000)
$7,500 to $10,699	29,000	77,000	56,000	162,000
($730 to $1,419)	(60,000)	(66,000)	(4,000)	(130,000)
$10,700 to $16,199	41,000	112,000	79,000	232,000
($1,420 to $3,079)	(37,000)	(34,000)	(3,000)	(74,000)
$16,200 and over	41,000	122,000	122,000	285,000
($3,080 and over)	(18,000)	(9,000)	(1,000)	(28,000)
Totals	163,000	407,000	311,000	881,000
	(281,000)	(265,000)	(23,000)	(569,000)

*The classification of college enrollees and nonenrollees was made by multiplying the number of high school graduates in each cell (Table 1) times the probability of college attendance obtained from Project TALENT and reported in Robert H. Berls, "Higher Education Opportunity and Achievement in the United States," *The Economics and Financing of Higher Education in the United-States,* a compendium of papers submitted to the Joint Economic Committee, Congress of the United States, Washington, D.C.: U.S. Government Printing Office, 1969, p. 150. In order to maintain the shape of this enrollment distribution, and achieve a total male enrollment of 881,000 (projected by the U.S. Office of Education for first-time degree-credit enrollment) an upward multiplier adjustment of 1.11 to each cell was required. The numbers of those classified as not likely to enroll in college were estimated by subtracting college enrollees from the total (Table 1) high school graduates in each cell.

Table 4. Estimated Joint Distribution of United States Black Male High School Graduates, 1969–70: Verbal Scholastic Aptitude and Family Income.* Top Figure in Each Cell Represents Estimated Number of Students in College; Bottom (Parentheses) Figure Represents Estimated Number Not in College

Family Income (Possible Family Contribution to Son's College Costs)	Verbal Scholastic Aptitude Test Scores			
	200–299	300–449	450–800	Totals
Less than $4,600	8,800	3,100	400	12,300
(Less than $270)	(37,180)	(8,170)	(350)	(45,700)
$4,600 to $7,499	5,400	3,900	480	9,780
($270 to $729)	(15,920)	(6,110)	(190)	(22,220)
$7,500 to $10,699	4,900	4,500	920	10,320
($730 to $1,419)	(11,730)	(4,790)	(160)	(16,680)
$10,700 to $16,199	5,500	6,000	1,570	13,070
($1,420 to $3,079)	(6,670)	(3,130)	(30)	(9,830)
$16,200 and over	1,800	3,150	1,080	6,030
($3,080 and over)	(1,400)	(650)	(20)	(2,070)
Totals	26,400	20,650	4,450	51,500
	(72,900)	(22,850)	(750)	(96,500)

* Classification of black college enrollees and nonenrollees was made for Table 4 in a manner similar to that used for Table 3 above. However, the college freshman total to which the multiplier adjustment controlled, 51,500, was obtained by multiplying the number from Table 2 of black male high school graduates (148,000) times 34.8 percent, the proportion of black male high school graduates in 1965 who enrolled in college by February 1967 as reported by the U.S. Bureau of the Census in *Factors Related to High School Graduation and College Attendance: 1967*, Series P-20, No. 185 (July 11, 1969), p. 5. An upwards multiplier adjustment to each cell of 1.205 was necessary to achieve the control total. This suggests that if the control totals in Tables 3 and 4 are correct, a larger adjustment to the Project TALENT college-attendance probabilities was necessary for blacks than for all United States high school graduates, and therefore, that blacks of comparable test scores and family incomes attend college in higher proportion than do all high school graduates. This finding is corroborated in recent work published by Alice M. Rivlin, and by Dorothy M. Knoell. The total number of black male college freshmen, 51,500, is also somewhat higher than the 44,900 which would be derived using the 1969 norms reported from the American Council on Education (881,000 X 5.1% = 44,931), reported in John A. Creager, Alexander W. Astin, Robert F. Boruch, Alan E. Bayer and David E. Drew, "National Norms for Entering College Freshmen—Fall 1969," Office of Research, American Council on Education, Washington, D.C., 1970, p. 22.

Since students taking the test usually intend to go to college, further adjustment is necessary before one can say what the performance of all high school graduates would be. Sample surveys conducted by Educational Testing Service suggest that roughly 70 percent of all United States male high school graduates could score 300 or better on the verbal sections of the SAT, and about 25 percent 450 or better.)

Before discussing individual sectors in the table and what they may mean, one should pause briefly to consider what they do *not* say. First, they are calculated estimates resulting from the combination of two kinds of distributions — one for family incomes of families of 17-year-olds who were enrolled in high school or college, the other for the estimated verbal Scholastic Aptitude Test score performance of all high school seniors including all black high school seniors. It is possible that sampling errors within the distributions, errors in combining the distributions, and errors in projecting forward in time may mean that the figures presented in Tables 1 and 2 may be incorrect by as much as 15 or 20 percent, and in Tables 3 and 4 that the classification between college students and others may contain even larger errors of estimation. This renders them questionable for precise work, but probably not for the general purpose of this discussion.

Furthermore, although family income is the best available nationwide index of ability to pay for college education, and although verbal SAT scores are probably the best available nationwide *group* description of probable ability to do college work successfully, no one should draw the conclusion that *individual* ability to pay, or *individual* likelihood of satisfactory academic performance can be predicted sensibly merely by entering a two-variable table of this kind. It cannot be done and should not be attempted.

Verbal test scores say little about energy or stamina or common sense — all of which are desirable qualities in an individual, and all of which, given time and effort, can affect the quality of individual academic performance. Kitano and Miller (1970) recently surveyed the early experience of Educational Opportunity Programs in California. The low-income minority students admitted to the University of California — the ones who did not meet the normal academic requirements for admission — mostly were in satisfactory standing at the university a year later and some were doing excellent academic work. Most were selected, Kitano and Miller say, by program directors who had many applicants from whom they could choose only a few, and also had application files which permitted them to know about, and weigh heavily, factors such as unusual motivation and stamina. Admission committees at several selective private colleges and universities have found from experience that for either minority or other students, they can relax their usual test-score expectations in individual cases at admission time by as much as 150 or 200 points on the SAT, and so long as the candidates concerned have other unusual and offsetting personal strengths, it usually turns out that what would otherwise have seemed to be a dangerous academic gamble was not much of a gamble at all.

But if one holds roughly constant these other and offsetting strengths, and examines the college academic performance of large groups, verbal aptitude measurement is far from meaningless. For one thing, verbal aptitude test scores describe ability to read almost as accurately as do scores on reading tests themselves. A verbal SAT score of 370 equals roughly the average performance of all United States high school seniors, while a verbal score of 250 — if achieved by a high school senior, would translate to measured reading competence at roughly the eighth- or ninth-grade level. For another thing, there is little evidence that suggests the Scholastic Aptitude Test is racially biased in the following specific sense: in a given college or group of colleges, a group of black students is likely to achieve roughly the same college grades in comparable courses as a group of white students who achieved the same SAT test scores prior to admission.[1]

If one turns back to the tables, a number of elements emerge quickly. Look first at the lower right-hand cells in Tables 3 and 4, at the students with high test scores who come from the most prosperous families (those scoring 450 or better on the SAT and from families earning $10,700 or more). Compared to the total number of high school graduates in each table, the numbers in these two cells seem unexpectedly small: they total roughly 14 percent of all United States male high school graduates, and 5 percent of the black male high school graduates.

This national college-candidate pool which one might define as bright enough to do good work at relatively selective colleges and prosperous enough to pay their tuition and other costs (without additional financial aid), is much smaller than generally imagined.

True, there are more high school graduates today than there were 5 or 10 years ago, and hence there are more students who submit college admissions applications that show good grade records and aptitude test results. Family incomes have risen, so that more of these students ought to be able to pay

1. S. A. Kendrick, "The Coming Segregation of Our Selective Colleges," *College Board Review,* Winter 1967–68, Vol. 66, pp. 6–13. The assertion in the text is limited and specific. It does not touch the broader questions of whether the variety of programs available in U.S. colleges is appropriate to the immediate needs of the minority/poverty students who do not now attend college—but who might if money and appropriate programs were available—or whether, within our college programs, different measures of performance should be devised that place less emphasis upon traditionally required verbal and mathematical skills.

higher tuition and other college costs than in prior years. But at the same time, in college after college, tuition fees and other charges have kept pace with the rise in family incomes, while at the same time the aptitude test score patterns (particularly the *minimum* score levels colleges consider admissible) have risen much more rapidly than the nation's supply of students with high test scores is growing. The effect of these latter trends in many of the most academically demanding colleges has been to cut back the effective size of the potential candidate pool of nonscholarship students, as these colleges have defined their pools through their fee schedules and admissions requirements. Meanwhile, by competing successfully for students within this unexpectedly small portion of the market, these relatively competitive colleges have had increasingly severe effect—more than they imagined—upon the ability of less competitive colleges to enroll relatively able and relatively prosperous students. These stringent developments, in turn, mean that both the financial plans and also the hopes for academic experiment and improvement in many other private colleges face a more difficult future than those colleges had imagined. The hopes for significant growth of private-college student aid programs for low-income students are limited by these same circumstances, unless new sources of funds become available. It is hardly surprising therefore, that relatively prosperous students with high test scores are being recruited with increasing intensity, and that most of them now do enroll in college.

Look next at the upper right-hand cells in Tables 3 and 4, students scoring 450 or better but from families with annual incomes less than $7,500. Some college officials, noting the increasing difficulty in recruiting full-paying students with high test scores, have suggested that if only their colleges had more scholarship money available, a large new market sector would be open to them, and that their institutions could then meet their hoped-for academic standards (as far as those are expressed in test measurements) and at the same time avoid making adjustments in the pace or design of curriculum. The relatively small numbers of students described in these particular cells in the tables, suggest that more scholarship money alone is not the answer. Only 5 percent of the high school graduates in Table 3 are found in this particular portion of the table, and three quarters of them already are college-bound within a year of high school graduation; only 1 percent of the black male high school graduates are in this portion of Table 4, and roughly two-thirds of them already are college-bound.

The nation's largest unsolved educational and social problem in higher education is illustrated in the upper left-hand corner of the tables—the sizable groups of students with average and below-average measured aptitude who also require substantial financial aid if they are to attend any college. In Table 3, the two cells that estimate the number of male high school graduates scoring between 200 and 300 on the verbal sections of the SAT and coming from families earning $7,500 or less, show that 166,000 of these students (91,000 plus 75,000) are not likely to enroll in college; this number, in turn, represents about 29 percent of all those not enrolling and about 11 percent of all United States male high school graduates.

The summary for black male high school graduates in Table 4 is even more severe. The same two cells in this table describe 53,100 (37,180 plus 15,920) black male high school graduates who are not likely to enroll in college within a year of high school graduation. This represents nearly a third of all of the United States male high school graduates jointly described in this way. It also represents more than half the black male graduates who do not go on to college and more than a third of the total number of black male high school graduates.

Issues Raised in the Tables

Of what practical use are large-group descriptive tables such as these? Why should one wish to classify young men and women as to family income and verbal aptitude test scores? Haven't we already overemphasized aptitude tests and overused their results? I persist in describing these groupings because I believe they provide a different kind of perspective for questions that face both colleges and students, and that demand clearer discussion than has occurred so far. My viewpoint is only one of many possible ones; for complicated questions, however, the consideration of many viewpoints seems clearly worth the extra effort.

One difficult question which requires clearer discussion is the level of funding and optimum design for state and federal supplementary programs of college student aid. If one can demonstrate clearly that a large number of the students who should be encouraged to attend college are accurately described as low-income and with relatively undeveloped reading skills, we should then be in a far better position to argue forcefully these conclusions:

1. A massive program of student loans, while it makes relatively small current demands on taxpayers and may seem initially like an attractive way to broaden opportunity, is nonetheless not likely to be very effective for these purposes. Surveys completed by Joseph D. Boyd and Robert H. Fenske (1969) at the Illinois State Scholarship Commission, and by Dorothy M. Knoell (1970) for the American Association of Junior Colleges, are among many which suggest that student loans may prove a helpful supplement to grants for low-income students. Student loans may also increase the freedom with which middle- and upper-income students choose among different kinds of colleges. But if they are the only form of new available aid, they probably will not attract large

numbers of low-income students into college who previously thought they could not afford it. Tables 3 and 4 demonstrate that of the students not now going to college, the low-income ones represent by far the largest number. If this had been more widely understood, perhaps President Nixon, in announcing recently a major new loan program (combined with only modest increases in grants), might have been less tempted to suggest that his proposals for 1970 would create quick, effective, and universal opportunity for higher education.

2. Financial aid program designers, pressed for funds, are also sometimes tempted to emphasize student employment which must be undertaken along with a regular academic program. The available evidence suggests that too great reliance already may be placed on student employment, particularly in the public two-year colleges. Furthermore, Tables 3 and 4 demonstrate that the largest number of potential college enrollees, if they enroll in currently available programs or anything like them, do not possess the reading facility to be able both to cope with the regular academic demands and also to spend long hours working to pay their expenses.

3. The evidence in the tables thus reinforces the notion that grants, such as the Educational Opportunity Grants, given in proportion to individual financial need, appear to be the most effective — if also the most expensive — financial incentive to encourage students to go on to college who otherwise would not do so. That conclusion, not apparently a popular one today, needs all the reinforcement it can get.

Several estimates have been produced recently concerning the aggregate financial need new federal programs should attempt to meet. The Carnegie Commission on Higher Education recommended that the federal government appropriate roughly $1 billion for Educational Opportunity Grants to needy students, supplemented by cost-of-education allowances to institutions, beginning in the academic year 1970–71. Alice D. Rivlin, then Assistant Secretary of the United States Department of Health, Education, and Welfare, prepared a report to the president in 1969 recommending appropriation of $2 billion for the same purpose (not including cost-of-education allowances for institutions), beginning in 1971–72. The tables presented here, combined with other information provided by the College Scholarship Service, suggests that the Rivlin proposal may be more realistic in educational terms, even if it may not be so in political ones.

Following a procedure commonly used in surveying state financial aid needs, James E. Nelson and Edward Sanders of the College Board (1970) have calculated the aggregate financial aid "deficit" for undergraduates enrolled in all United States colleges in the current year. They have calculated the total out-of-pocket costs these students must meet in the colleges they attend, have estimated the distribution of students' family incomes in those colleges — and from this have calculated the amounts which families in normal circumstances should be expected to contribute to help meet these costs — and have also estimated the other sources of financial aid (except for summer earnings) which in aggregate were available to students at various income levels. Defined this way, and assuming arbitrarily that students on the average can save $400 apiece each year from summer earnings toward their college expenses, Nelson and Sanders would estimate a deficit of about $1.7 billion — representing "overcontribution" by students and their families in excess of what one should expect from the normal CSS calculations. (For perspective, the total out-of-pocket college expense bill to be paid by undergraduates in 1969–70 under the Sanders-Nelson calculations is about $11 billion, of which about $3 billion now comes from institutional, state, and federal sources in the form of scholarships, loans, and jobs, and of which the remainder is provided by students and their families.) The degree to which the CSS standard family contribution tables are generous or stringent obviously affects how large a deficit is calculated. The tables used in the current calculations are significantly more generous to families than they were as recently as 1966; use of the old tables might well have eliminated any calculated aggregate deficit for 1969–70.

This aggregate approach, however, assumes that the available financial support is distributed evenly and where it is needed; we know this is not the case. If we were able to collect information about aid deficits, college by college, the resulting figure — which would take explicit account of maldistribution of funds — would surely be much larger. However, the overcontribution by enrolled students and by their families is only part of the picture. Some would say it is the least important part, since at least the overcontributing students are attending college somehow.

Tables 3 and 4 enable one to make rough guesses also about the amount of financial need among students who are *not* in college, but might be if they had financial help. Part of Dorothy Knoell's recent survey, *People Who Need College* (1970), included interviews with more than 400 black high school graduates in each of five cities (Dallas, Forth Worth, St. Louis, San Francisco, and Philadelphia) — recent graduates who did not plan to attend college. Roughly 37 percent said the primary reason they did not plan to continue formal education was lack of money. The amounts of additional money they estimated they needed in order to continue formal education ranged from $1,000 a year to $2,000. In 1968 the State Council on Higher Education for Virginia asked each guidance counselor in the state how many of their students that year failed to go on to college solely because they lacked money, and how much money they thought was needed. The counselors, in sum, estimated that about 14 percent of those not continuing their education failed to do so for lack of money, and that the average amount needed per year per student was about $1,200. It is difficult to estimate a precise national percentage for those who are diverted from further education because they lack money, partly because a student's reason for continuing or not continuing education usually is a mixture of many reasons. Furthermore, the amount of need per student depends on which kind of college appears to be the most realistic possibility. The estimate a student would make if thinking seriously about living at home and attending a community college is different from his estimate if he hopes to attend a private college away from home. These uncertainties acknowledged, it is still possible to make reasonable assumptions that will serve for initial projections. From Tables 3 and 4 one estimates that in 1969, 569,000 United States male high school graduates, of whom 96,500 are black, will not go on to college within a year of graduation from high school. Most of these students come from families where they can expect little or no financial help. If one estimates that each student who does decide to go on to higher education will need an average of $1,500 a year, then one can set up the following equation to estimate additional student aid needed — predominantly in the form of need-based grants — in order to stimulate significant improvement in the college attendance rate. One can estimate that the number of male high school graduates *not* going on to college, times 50 percent times $1,500 needed per student per year, times two (producing an estimate for both men and women), times three (a rough multiplier to allow eventually for paying for not just the freshman class, but for four undergraduate classes that have gone through roughly normal attrition along the way) equals aid needed to increase college going as much as feasible by this method. Estimated this way, the current additional need is $3.5 billion a year for all high school graduates. There would still remain 284,500 high school graduates each year who do not go on to college, but these presumably are the ones who are not seriously deterred by lack of money now, if the calculations above were made using the correct beginning assumptions. Included in that total estimate, there is need for $434 million a year, to reduce by half the number of black high school graduates who now fail to go on to college.

In the formula above, one of the most obvious skeptical questions one might ask is whether 50 percent is too high an estimate of the proportion of high school graduates who fail to attend college because they lack money. A conservative guess, supported by several, but by no means all, of the available surveys, might be as low as 20 percent or less. However, one should also remember that the number of secondary school students who are actually graduated is not necessarily a fixed element in the equation. If secondary schools improve in quality, particularly the weaker ones, and if some of the new special programs designed to increase high school retention rates prove successful, and if more money is made available to low-income college students primarily on the basis of financial need, then the number of high school graduates in any year will be greater than one would project today under present conditions. Robert H. Berls (1969), at the Bureau of Higher Education in the United States Office of Education, has estimated recently that almost 20 percent of all high school entrants and almost 40 percent of black high school entrants do not graduate from high school. If, for example, these high school dropout rates were cut in half, this would add 181,000 male high school graduates to the 1969–70 totals in Tables 1 and 3, and about 50,000 black male high school graduates to the totals in Tables 2 and 4. The generosity of the 50 percent in the formula helps adjust, in an extremely rough way, for these kinds of possibilities.

Most high school guidance counselors would say that student financial aid for entering freshmen ought to be committed (or known to be available) when the student involved is still in high school — particularly if one of the main purposes of that aid is to encourage going to college. At this stage, however, unless one is a skilled mind reader, it is impossible to know whether, if a high school senior *didn't* get aid, he or she would still go on to college. Yet without knowing this answer ahead of time, one cannot avoid giving aid to needy students, many of whom would have gone on to college anyway — whether or not they received aid. Thus, the practical design of any student aid program designed to broaden opportunity must take into account *both* kinds of deficits calculated earlier: overcontribution by presently enrolled students and their families, and also the cost of bringing in new students who are presently outside our system of higher education. In the example above, the combined annual deficit for all undergraduates would be $5.2 billion ($1.7 billion plus $3.5 billion), and within that total, for black undergraduates, an estimated $800 million.

Clearly, the calculation has many imprecise elements. One may hope that better data may soon be available to improve their precision. Detail for the calculations has been provided here, not to imply any final accuracy, but to illustrate the major variables such a calculation must account for, and to show the rough size of the costs which result.

With an end to the war in Southeast Asia not yet foreseeable, and with other demands for public expenditure increasing at the same time, it seems probable that Congress and the state legislatures, in sum, will not vote major new current appropriations of this size for college-student financial aid, and that the formation of public policy in this area for at least the next two or three years will be characterized by persistent attempts to achieve inherently expensive educational results at bargain prices. In any enterprise as complex as undergraduate financial aid, however, bargain-price tags often carry hidden costs and hidden problems. I expect that the following will prove to be only the beginning of a list of apparently attractive solutions that seem more attractive at first glance than they will if uncritically pursued and put into practice.

1. Student loans and educational opportunity. Enlarged use of student loans in the last decade clearly has stretched the effectiveness of increasingly tight institutional and government scholarship budgets, has eased students' personal problems in budgeting for college, and in some instances has provided these students greater flexibility of college choice. Loans provide the quickest way to expand student purchasing power at the lowest current-appropriation cost to taxpayers. Attractive-sounding arguments have been made that borrowing to attend college can be put on an equitable basis (for example, by varying repayment rates according to individuals' lifetime earning rates) and that, on the average, loans represent an investment in higher earning power that any young American ought to be glad to make. However, if the present and growing student aid deficit is met *primarily* through student loans, we will have also succeeded in shifting much of the cost of undergraduate education from the older generations to the student generation, we may well have distorted patterns of career choice and marriage, and we probably will have done little to encourage low-income students of all races to attend college in larger proportions than they do now.

2. Funding levels and freedom to choose. If one has only limited funds available and wants to stretch them as far as possible, another attractive economy is to set the level of student subsidy as low as reasonably possible. Usually this means setting it at a level that will permit a needy student to attend a two-year, or perhaps a four-year public college. The president's student financial aid proposals for 1970 appear to have followed this pattern. If the federal government and state governments consistently pursue this policy, however, a number of side-effects become increasingly probable. For one thing, individual students will have less freedom to choose the kinds of college they feel are most appropriate for them. In Illinois, one of the few states where the state scholarship and grant programs give significantly greater allowances to students attending expensive colleges, the State Scholarship Commission asked award recipients in 1967–68 how their educational plans would have changed if they had not received state awards. Of the students receiving need-based grants, 92 percent were white and 6 percent were black. The grants averaged about $700 each, and were awarded with only minimum academic requirements: that the recipient be a high school graduate and admitted to college. Six out of 10 of the whites and 8 out of 10 of the blacks enrolled in private four-year colleges in Illinois. One quarter of all the grant recipients, and 4 out of 10 of the black students said that if they had not received the Illinois state award they would not have enrolled in college at all, but instead would have taken a job or enlisted in one of the military services.[2]

If student aid is largely awarded on the basis of financial need, it is clear that the least expensive student-aid bill can be achieved for any given number of students if the rich ones attend expensive colleges and the low-income ones attend the least expensive colleges. This extreme solution, however, is poor educational policy and poor social policy. Under today's conditions, it is also poor economic policy. Many private colleges are operating at less than full capacity, while most public colleges are under severe pressure to provide new places. Public legislative bodies may imagine they save money by not giving students extra aid to attend more expensive colleges; but if taxpayers are also forced to provide new public-college places, and to pay for the cost of education in excess of the usually low tuition fees prevailing in these colleges, then the total public bill will be seriously understated if merely the financial aid costs are presented and discussed.

Finally, the shift in enrollment balance from private to public colleges is occurring at unprecedented speed. In 1968, for the first peacetime year in this century, enrollment in private colleges actually declined. In recent years, 10 new students enrolled in public colleges for every new student in private colleges. As recently as 1950, roughly half the nation's college students were enrolled in private or church-related colleges. By 1985, this ratio may be something like one-fifth private to four-fifths public. If pluralism in the control of American higher education is a useful element of strength in its structure, that quality and strength is now diminishing rapidly. Perhaps this is an unavoidable side effect of necessary public spending policy, but it is rarely discussed in these terms, and it should be.

3. Educational opportunity and curriculum. Partly because of the different complexity of the problems involved, and partly because of the way our colleges and universities are governed, it is simpler to change admission policy and even financial aid policy than it is to design, test, and introduce new curriculums. As educational opportunity is broadened to include groups of students who did not formerly attend college, it will be increasingly important to try to keep educational programs sensibly responsive to these new admissions patterns. The educational programs must make a worthwhile difference to the students enrolling in them, or the phrase ''educational opportunity'' will lose its

---

2. Unpublished data provided by Dr. Joseph D. Boyd, Executive Director, Illinois State Scholarship Commission, Deerfield, Illinois.

meaning. Stated this vaguely, there is little new in the idea. It is mentioned here to emphasize that the financial aid costs estimated above are far from the only ones which must concern us if we are to produce changes that have long-run value.

4. Fair allocation of insufficient funds. When money is in short supply compared with growing and legitimate demand for it, questions of equity and of political strategy to achieve equity become much more difficult. The abrasion caused by sharply different pricing structures in public and private colleges seems more intense, and the temptation grows greater for each sector to press its own case, rather than one which might more nearly represent a consensus of all sectors. Minority groups come under more severe pressure to choose whether to take an adversary position towards colleges and legislatures, so as to try to obtain a larger share of presently available funds, or to join with the college and university community in pressing for allocation of a larger share of the nation's income to education generally.

One particularly urgent question of allocation, I believe, is posed by the changes that have occurred since 1966 in the College Scholarship Service tables, used by more than 500 colleges for estimating the contribution a family is expected to provide for a son's or daughter's education. The following summary shows the reduction in expected family contribution for normal-budget, three-child families, when the 1966 tables are compared with the most recent ones.

Pre-Tax Family Income	Contribution Expected by CSS Pre-1966 Tables	Contribution Expected by CSS under Tables Used for 1970 Freshman Stipends	Amount by Which Expected Contribution Is Reduced
$ 5,000	$ 340	—	$340
10,000	1,250	$ 740	510
15,000	2,650	1,690	960

There are several results of this change. Individual students receiving need-based scholarships (and their families) obtain welcome relief from some of the demands which would have been placed upon them four years ago. Private colleges, feeling increased pressure from the low tuition pricing at public colleges, are now in a slightly better position to compete for middle-income students while still following a policy of awarding no more scholarship aid than a standard calculation of need permits. However, the funds that would pay for five scholarships a few years ago, pay for only four comparable scholarships today — solely on account of the changes in the tables and before considering the effects of inflation. Because scarce dollars cannot be stretched as far as they used to be, it has become harder for many private colleges to admit more minority/poverty students. The few who were admitted and aided have benefited from the change; but other students, sometimes low-income ones, sometimes middle-income ones, have lost opportunities because of the change. Did these alterations produce more beneficial effects than harmful ones, whatever the statistical reasons may have been for the change? If not, shouldn't the tables be tightened a bit, particularly, perhaps, at the middle-income levels, at least until the present period of extreme financial stringency has eased somewhat?

Conclusion

Until more money becomes available for college student financial aid, it appears that in fairness to the many we should be extremely cautious about granting extra relief to the few. I believe we should reexamine the css family contribution tables, to see if it is not possible to allocate the scholarship funds of the member css colleges more broadly, while still being fair to individual students and their families.

Meanwhile, the most important financial aid issue today, and one critical to broadening the availability of college education, is whether or not significant amounts of new money can be made available to finance the obvious needs, in ways that will meet those needs without producing severe and unwanted side effects. The recommendations of the Carnegie Commission on Higher Education and of the Rivlin Report show the direction I believe we should support most strongly for undergraduate student aid. Until these recommendations, or ones like them, become reality, colleges and students are in for a series of uncommonly lean years.

References

Berls, Robert H., "Higher Education Opportunity and Achievement in the United States," p. 197 in *The Economics and Financing of Higher Education in the United States.* A compendium of papers submitted to the Joint Economic Committee, Congress of the United States. Washington, D.C.: U.S. Government Printing Office, 1969.

Boyd, Joseph D., and Fenske, Robert H., *A Study of 1967–68 Scholarship and Grant Recipients.* Deerfield, Ill.: Illinois State Scholarship Commission, 1969, 138 pp.

Fields, Cheryl M., "Nixon's Legislative Plans Called 'Little Help' to Colleges," *The Chronicle of Higher Education,* May 18, 1970, p. 7.

Kitano, Harry H. L., and Miller, Dorothy L., *An Assessment of Educational Opportunity Programs in California Higher Education.* San Francisco: Scientific Analysis Corporation, 1970, pp. 24–25, 58. Mimeographed.

Knoell, Dorothy M., *People Who Need College: A Report on Students We Have Yet to Serve.* Washington, D.C.: American Association of Junior Colleges, 1970.

Sanders, Edward, and Nelson, James E., "Financing of Undergraduates, 1969–70," *Financial Aid News,* Vol. 10, No. 2, July 1970.

State Council of Higher Education for Virginia, *A Study of Student Financial Aid in Virginia.* Richmond, Va.: The Council, 1969, pp. 21–23.

Colloquium Participants[1]

Alexander W. Astin
  Director of Research, American Council on Education, Washington, D.C.
Helen S. Astin
  Director of Research, University Research Corporation, Washington, D.C.
Allan B. Ballard Jr.
  University Dean for Academic Development, The City University of New York, New York, New York
Lawrence V. Barclay
  Program Associate, College Entrance Examination Board, New York, New York
David Boubion
  Dean of Students, California State College, Los Angeles, California
Vincent J. Browne
  Dean of Liberal Arts, Howard University, Washington, D.C.
Broadus N. Butler
  President, Dillard University, New Orleans, Louisiana
Kenneth B. Clark
  President, Metropolitan Applied Research Center, Inc., New York, New York
Fred E. Crossland
  Program Officer, The Ford Foundation, New York, New York
Addie Crutcher
  Project Director, Educational Talent Search, Miles College, Birmingham, Alabama
Margaret Dagen
  Associate Director of Admissions, Washington University, St. Louis, Missouri
William L. Dandridge
  Staff Associate, National Association of Independent Schools, Boston, Massachusetts
Lorraine B. Dennis
  Department of Psychology, Roger Williams College, Providence, Rhode Island
Harrison F. deShields
  Director of Admissions, Bethune Cookman College, Daytona Beach, Florida
Humphrey Doermann
  Assistant Dean for Financial Affairs, Harvard University, Cambridge, Massachusetts
Eunice L. Edwards
  Director of Financial Aids, Fisk University, Nashville, Tennessee
David L. Evans
  Associate Director of Admissions, Harvard University, Cambridge, Massachusetts

---

1. Affiliations shown are those that were current at the time of the colloquium.

John K. Folger
    Executive Director, Tennessee Higher Education Commission, Nashville, Tennessee
Edmund W. Gordon
    Chairman, Department of Guidance, Teachers College, Columbia University, New York, New York
Robert K. Hage
    Director of Financial Aid, Dartmouth College, Hanover, New Hampshire
George H. Hanford
    Acting President, College Entrance Examination Board, New York, New York
Timothy S. Healy
    Vice Chancellor for Academic Affairs. The City University of New York, New York, New York
Benjamin J. Henley
    Acting Superintendent, District of Columbia Public Schools, Washington, D.C.
Watts W. Hill Jr.
    Member, North Carolina State Board of Higher Education, Durham, North Carolina
William I. Ihlandfelt
    Director of Admissions, Northwestern University, Evanston, Illinois
Jane W. Jacqz
    Secretary, African-American Institute, New York, New York
Samuel Johnson
    Director, National Scholarship Service and Fund for Negro Students, Atlanta, Georgia
H. Paul Kelley
    Director, Measurement and Evaluation Center, University of Texas, Austin, Texas
S. A. Kendrick
    Executive Director of Research, College Entrance Examination Board, New York, New York
Hugh W. Lane
    President, National Scholarship Service and Fund for Negro Students, New York, New York
Frank A. Logan
    Director of Admissions, Antioch College, Yellow Springs, Ohio
Winton H. Manning
    Director, Developmental Research, Educational Testing Service, Princeton, New Jersey
Sam A. McCandless
    Director for the Commission on Tests, College Entrance Examination Board, New York, New York

John D. Millett
Chancellor, Ohio Board of Regents, Columbus, Ohio
Joseph S. Murphy
Vice Chancellor, New Jersey Department of Higher Education, Trenton, New Jersey
Louis Nuñez
National Executive Director, ASPIRA of America, New York, New York
Charles D. O'Connell Jr.
Dean of Students, University of Chicago, Chicago, Illinois
Ruben C. Pardo
Assistant Director, Educational Opportunity Program, California State College, Long Beach
John Peper
Acting Director, Research and Evaluation Department, School District of Philadelphia, Pennsylvania
Filor Phifer
Director of Admissions, Livingston College, Rutgers—The State University of New Jersey, New Brunswick, New Jersey
Hollace G. Roberts
Acting Vice President, College Entrance Examination Board, New York, New York
Frank Sandage
Director of Talent Search, Morehead State University, Morehead, Kentucky
William G. Shannon
Associate Executive Director, American Association of Junior Colleges, Washington, D.C.
Sally Smith
Co-Director, Nairobi Talent Search, Nairobi College, Nairobi, California
Julian C. Stanley
Professor of Psychology, The Johns Hopkins University, Baltimore, Maryland
C. Sumner Stone
Director, Educational Opportunities Projects, Educational Testing Service, Princeton, New Jersey
B. Alden Thresher
Director of Admissions Emeritus, Massachusetts Institute of Technology, Cocoa Beach, Florida
Edmund C. Toomey
Dean of Students, St. Louis University, St. Louis, Missouri
William W. Turnbull
Executive Vice President, Educational Testing Service, Princeton, New Jersey

John A. Valentine
  Executive Director of Examinations, College Entrance Examination Board, New York, New York
Clyde Vroman
  Director of Admissions, University of Michigan, Ann Arbor, Michigan
Warren W. Willingham
  Senior Research Psychologist, College Entrance Examination Board, Palo Alto, California
Stephen J. Wright
  Consultant to the President, College Entrance Examination Board, New York, New York

DATE DUE